M000164895

THE ISLES OF GREECE

A Collection of the Poetry of Place

Edited by
JOHN LUCAS

ELAND • LONDON

First published in 2010 by Eland Publishing Ltd
61 Exmouth Market, Clerkenwell, London EC1R 4QL

ISBN 978 1 906011 16 1

Pages designed and typeset by Antony Gray
Cover image: Detail from the Dolphin Frescoes in the
Queen's bathroom, Palace of Minos (1600–1400BC) /
Giraudon / Bridgeman Art Library
Printed and bound in Spain by GraphyCems, Navarra

Contents

INTRODUCTION

Ocean cartographers have always had difficulty in mapping islands. The difficulties fall into two major categories. Do particular islands exist at all, and if so, where exactly are they? According to Robert Macfarlane, 'Nineteenth-century British admiralty charts included more than two hundred islands that are now known not to exist.' And according to a BBC producer I occasionally worked with, and who had a passion for sailing single-handed across the Atlantic and was paid to deliver yachts from boatyards on the Solent to wealthy owners in Florida, some of the smaller islands in the Bermuda Triangle had different trig references on different charts, and these could vary by as much as three-quarters of a nautical mile. Given this, it seems to me less remarkable that ancient Greek map-makers charting the Mediterranean committed mistakes than that they got so much right. Of course, there were errors. They identified islands for which there now seems no evidence, though some may well have been blown out of the water or sunk by volcanoes and earthquakes. (Most geologists agree that the vast explosion *circa* 1500 BC which destroyed much of Minoan civilisation also shattered a large land mass and turned Crete and Santorini into separate islands.) According to both Hesiod (eighth century BC) and Pindar (c.520–440 BC), the fertile Islands of the Blest lay to the west beyond the Pillars of Hercules – that is, Gibraltar – and were peopled by the virtuous dead who lived in perpetual bliss. Tennyson's Ulysses urges his companions to join him on a last sea voyage in which they 'may touch the happy Isles,/And see the great Achilles, whom we knew'.

Paul Harvey suggests that reports about the existence of these places may have come from mariners who had reached islands off the west coast of Africa. Other mariners brought back tales of islands which were sent hither and thither by winds or which chose to float freely of their own sweet will. Delos, according to Pindar, was originally one such island and became tethered to the floor of the Mediterranean only after Zeus chose it for the birthplace of Artemis and Apollo, whose mother, Leto, had to be protected from Hera's jealousy. 'Delos' means in ancient Greek 'which has come to light from', and in his short ode to the island, Pindar writes of how

> Shifted about in times past
> by waves and contrary winds,
> when the Titans' daughter
> laboured ashore in her last
> child-bearing convulsions,
> four iron-girthed pillars rose
> from the unplumbable deeps to hold
> this rock-island on their capitals . . .

Anyone who has voyaged on the Aegean and watched as a Greek island emerges uncertainly out of blue haze will be likely to agree that there is something ethereal about the slow thickening of the atmosphere before it hardens to a rocky outline. Glyn Hughes puts this as well as anyone when, in some lines to be more fully quoted later, he recalls seeing Greek islands 'floating on rainbows above a rim of surf', as if they are 'caught in the act of their descent,/not rocks from out of the sea'; sea surface full of clouds solidified to earth where 'Paradisal green/Gave suavity to the perplexed machine/Of ocean . . . ', to quote Wallace Stevens.

Stevens's playfulness is a triumph of the poetic imagination, its verbal conjurings. Such imagination has always been at its most intense when confronted with the magic of the Aegean, although very few of the great modern poets actually visited Greece. Like their predecessors of many centuries, they preferred Italy. That 'broken dandy' Byron was the first great English-speaking poet of modern times to go there. Milton had intended to go on to Sicily and then Greece from Italy, through which he was journeying in 1638–9, but news of the outbreak of the Civil War recalled him to England. Later, however, when he came to write *Paradise Lost,* he recalled the moment in Homer when Hephaestos is lobbed from heaven by Zeus, though he Latinises the names to Mulciber and Jove in mythographising the fall of Satan. Mulciber, he says, is pitched out

> . . . by angry Jove
> Sheer o'er the crystal battlements; from morn
> To noon he fell, from noon to dewy eve,
> A summer's day; and with the setting sun
> Dropped from the zenith like a falling star,
> On Lemnos the Aegean isle . . .

And having written these breathtaking lines, Milton characteristically adds that the tale so told is wrong, 'for he with his rebellious rout/Fell long before'. Lemnos or modern-day Limnos (Milton would have preferred the earlier spelling because it makes for that lovely tumbling link of assonance falling through the lines from 'fell' through 'setting' and 'zenith' to 'Lemnos' itself) is the island associated with Hephaestos, its capital city in classical times being called Hephaestia. In post-classical times it was occupied by the Venetians, then the Turks, and only brought under Greek control in 1912. As if that wasn't enough, Lemnos was where Agamemnon left Philoctetes, whose cries from the suppurating ankle wound caused by a serpent so distressed his fellow voyagers that they abandoned him on the then-uninhabited island. (Later they had to rescue him so that, according to prophecy, he could kill Paris with his spear and the Greeks could then defeat the Trojans).

Hardly any of those young Englishmen who made the Grand Tour in the seventeenth and eighteenth centuries bothered with such stuff, any more than they bothered with Greece itself. Its glory lay in the past. The present was ruins. Perhaps for this reason, Greece could be imagined only in terms of idyll, of Theocritan shepherds and country maids, of the Vale of Tempe. Nor could Greek poets help correct this partial vision, for the good reason that over a long period there weren't any. C. A. Trypanis's major anthology, *The Penguin Book of Greek Verse,* covers fourteen centuries in fewer than a hundred pages (including translations). Leave aside Byzantine hymns and folk songs – these latter attractive but largely confined to ballads about love – and there is barely anything of substance, and certainly nothing about Greece itself, until the moment when the movement for Greek liberation from Turkish rule begins at the end of the eighteenth century. Among the harbingers of this movement are the Klephtic ballads, which Trypanis doesn't include, and the work of the first two distinctively modern Greek poets, Andreas Kalvos (1792–1869) and Dionysios Solomos (1798–1857), which he does. Solomos, whose *Songs of Greece,* written in demotic Greek, established him as Greece's national poet, was born on Zante and lived much of his time there or on neighbouring Corfu. Kalvos, also born on Zante, was in exile for much of his life. He wrote a poem for his native island, remarkable for high-flown imagery which he derived, I think, from the great Spanish poet Gongora, and Ugo Foscola, with whom Kalvos was on good terms and whom he followed from Italy into Swiss exile – 'You, when night casts over the roses of the sky her darkest veil, you are the only joy in my dreams'; but as Kalvos wrote in a strange compound of neo-classical Greek and a diction of his own making, the soldiers he hoped his poems would inspire couldn't understand a word of them. Anyway, Kalvos's identification of Zante as an earthly paradise hardly squares with the fact that the isles of Greece are also places of tragic history, from the cruel exploits of the gods through to the late twentieth century, from Homer to the Colonels. And while different islands may not have wandered from one spot to another they have from time to time been annexed by different powers: Venice, Turkey, Italy and Germany among them. This inevitably produces a sense of floating or shifting identity in many island dwellers. Some years ago my wife and I were staying for a few days on the island of Leros with the distinguished Greek–Australian poet Dimitris Tsaloumas. When Dimitris was born there in 1921, the island, which is one of the Dodecanese, was under Italian control. In 1943 it came briefly into the possession of the British who were then pushed off it by the Germans. Only after 1945 did it become Greek owned, a fact which its older inhabitants often found difficult to grasp. 'The day after you leave,' Dimitris told us, 'I have to go to Greece.' He meant that he had to go to Athens.

Leros, while not the most favoured of Greek islands – it has had to overcome the post-war scandal of being used as a dumping-ground for the mentally ill – is full of scenic splendours. Tourists can appreciate these. But it is also notable for its separate cemeteries which house the bodies of Italian, Greek, German and British soldiers, sailors and airmen. And during the period of the civil war, and for years afterwards, neighbour was turned against neighbour. There were imprisonments, incriminations, recriminations, murders. And what is true of Leros is true of many Greek islands. They are as remarkable for their beauty as for their tragic histories. 'Wherever I travel Greece wounds me', the celebrated Greek poet, George Seferis, wrote in a poem of 1937. ' "Be not afeard; the isle is full of noises,/Sounds and sweet airs, that give delight, and hurt not," ' Caliban tells Trinculo and Stephano, who are on their way to commit murder, in Shakespeare's *The Tempest*. Such beauty and such cruelty. The townships of Greek islands, the white-painted *choras* in which the wandering tourist delights because of their labyrinthine ways, their winding, narrow passages doubling back on each other before darting off at weird up-and-down angles, where fishing nets dry in the sun and at evening old women, their day's work at an end, sit on doorsteps talking and laughing, were so constructed in order to confuse marauding corsairs intent on rape, robbery and slaughter.

*   *   *

When I sat down to compile this anthology, at first I thought I would follow Odysseus on his journey back from Troy to Ithaka, dropping in poems and pieces of prose as the journey progressed. But I soon realised that this wouldn't do, not merely because the exact course of the wily one's sea-route is to some extent a matter of conjecture, but because for all the islands he did visit there were many more he didn't. Greece is a country of over two thousand islands, and while most are uninhabited, this still leaves a large number which have been the birthplace of notable poets and which other poets, Greek and non-Greek, have visited and about which they have written. I have therefore assumed a sea journey starting from Athens's main port, Piraeus. What this leads to will, I hope, entertain, surprise and delight.

SAILING TO ISLANDS

It is possible nowadays to fly direct to certain Greek islands. But to go by aeroplane is to miss the dramas of departure and arrival by boat and, even more, the joy of the voyage. Most sea journeys start from Piraeus. Other ports serve a number of the Greek islands: from Patras and Igoumenitsa you can sail to Corfu and the Ionians; ferries from Volos and Thessaloniki serve the north Aegean islands and the Sporades. But Piraeus is where most travellers start from. Noisy, dirty, sprawling, the port is nevertheless not without allure, and not simply because of its association with bars where, amid the whiff of hashish and the presence of easy women, you could at one time listen to the forbidden music of *rembetika* and meet old sailors such as 'Captain Fletcher', commemorated by Nikos Kavvadias (1910–75) in a poem of the same name. At the head of it he explains: 'The German merchant captain Henry Fletcher ran the freighter *Scheld* aground off Matapan, the fog having for some days prevented his "bringing down" the sun with his sextant. He went mad, and died in Piraeus of sunstroke.' Kavvadias was himself a wireless operator on board various merchant ships, a self-made poet of the kind Greece so often throws up, as it does artists and musicians, and although he plays no further part in this anthology, his poems, in Simon Darragh's fine versions, are well worth seeking out.

Kavvadias was an habitué of Piraeus's waterfront bars, where, as he put it in one poem, 'shameless women catch the sailors', and in another, 'drugs are a slower way to die'. The bars are gone, the allure remains. After all, from here, as the different shipping lines and ferries proclaim, you can sail to virtually all points of the Aegean – from Lesbos in the north to Patmos and Rhodes due east, to the Cycladic islands of Paros, Naxos and Milos, and to Santorini and Crete in the south. Island Greece begins here.

> The isles of Greece! The isles of Greece!
>   Where burning Sappho loved and sung,
> Where grew the arts of war and peace,
>   Where Delos rose, and Phoebus sprung!
> Eternal summer gilds them yet,
> But all, except their sun, is set.
>
> The Scian* and the Teian* muse,
>   The hero's harp, the lover's lute,
> Have found the fame your shores refuse:
>   Their place of birth alone is mute
> To sounds that echo further west
> Than your sires' 'Islands of the Blest'.
>
> The mountains look on Marathon –
>   And Marathon looks on the sea;
> And musing there an hour alone,
>   I dreamed that Greece might still be free;
> For standing on the Persian's grave,
> I could not deem myself a slave.

These famous stanzas from Canto 3 of *Don Juan* are probably better known to Greeks than to English readers. They secured Byron (1788–1824) a lasting place in Greek affections, especially when coupled with his championing of the cause of Greek independence from Turkey. He had already addressed the subject in Canto 2 of *Childe Harold's Pilgrimage* (1812), a work based on his travels

---

* *Scian, Teian:* Homer (the harp) was reputed to have been born on the island of Chios, Anacreon (lute) at Teos, a town on the coast of Asia Minor.

through Europe and the Balkans, where he had mourned 'Fair Greece! sad relic of departed worth!/Immortal, though no more! though fallen, great!' but it was the encomium to the Isles of Greece that sealed his reputation with the Greeks and gave a phrase to the language which is as evocative as it is heady with incantatory power.

The headiness of expectation is beautifully caught in some lines by Glyn Hughes, poet and novelist, who lived in Greece for a few years during the 1970s and remembers that whenever he left Athens to sail towards islands:

> I was always taken by surprise
> by the first buds of them on the horizon
> breaking the calm pool of that blue,
> floating on rainbows above a rim of surf –
> as if caught in the act of their descent,
> not rocks from out of the sea.
> They were so still beneath their perfume-clouds
> of figs, oregano, and of thyme,
> they seemed deserted. Then the cliffs
> open and the noise of sailors,
> whose rhythms are the sea's, quick here, slow there,
> waiting, rushing, tells us we approach a pier.
> The boat grinds its iron and we disembark
> in the cacophony of those who importune
> with that Hellenic gesture – from the breast
> and open-palmed as if they held
> their hearts there, lightly though invisibly
> about to cast them on the receiving air . . .

Of course, this being the Aegean Sea, expectations can collide with the unexpected. The following poem, 'One for Zeno', is about an incident in which my wife and I, together with two Greek friends, were involved when, years ago, we sailed for Syros.

A mile out the propeller scraped on rock,
Though no real harm, it seemed – a jolting shock,
The sound of a dog's teeth working on bone,
Then we were safe in harbour, our trip done.

We'd sat below decks with a black-dressed woman,
Now crossing herself, who'd told us of her mission.
'The Blessed Virgin came to me last night, she
Pulled me from sleep, commanding, "Aphrodite,

Tomorrow make your pilgrimage to Tinos."
So I took ship. But I'll get off at Syros.
That struck propeller was a sign, I heard
It warning me against the Virgin's word.

It had my husband's voice, it said, "Trust no one
Who comes to give you orders in a vision."
He'll often appear to rasp out that command.
His word's my law. Pray God she'll understand.'

Zeno (c.460 BC) was the famous inventor of sets of seemingly
impossible paradoxes. On 15 August many Greeks go to Tinos to
celebrate the feast of the Assumption because in 1922 a sailor
claimed to have had a vision of the Virgin Mary on the island, one
given special force when, shortly afterwards, a small figurine of the
Virgin was found in a cleft of inaccessible rock.

A rather different bafflement of purpose occurs in 'Naxos' by
Iakovos Kampanelis, where an island disappoints by not being what
the visitor hopes for, its people failing in their responsibility to
Greekness.

We set off for Naxos on April the nineteenth
by the regular Saturday-afternoon steamer,

a crowd of private and public servants, embarking,
as I said, on Saturday afternoon,
paying God knows what for our passage.

We arrived after two hundred miles and maybe a dozen hours.
That is to say: we arrived
geographically speaking, or from what you might call
the ship's viewpoint, since after all
we'd squeezed every last inch out of our tickets . . .
but no Naxos!
And yet the chart insisted
that this port was Naxos,
and all the townsfolk swore: Damn our souls,
they said, if this isn't Naxos
and we its inhabitants.

We left, disappointed in Naxos and its people.

If only the fools who met us at the quay had had the brains
to reject who they were, and where,
that might have been the Naxos we hoped for.

In his Forward to *Ithaka: Modern Greek Poetry in Translation*, the short selection of translations from which this poem comes, the Australian poet, Martin Johnston (1947–90), who made his versions while Greece was suffering under the Junta, points out that some at least of the poems he has translated are by Greek poets 'who have not yet allowed totalitarianism to stifle their voices'. This is clearly the case with 'Naxos'. Its speaker is one of the idiots who belonged to or sympathised with the Junta, the stated ambition of which was to rescue Greece from itself, to 'put it in plaster'. The man's pettiness comes out in his determination to squeeze 'every last inch' out of his ticket, his contemptuous, and contemptible, attitude to the islanders in his belief in their provincial remoteness from Athens – Naxos is certainly *not* two hundred miles from Piraeus. Martin Johnston was the son of Charmian Clift and George Johnston, Australian writers who lived for several years in the 1950s and 1960s on the island of Hydra, having spent an initial year on Kalymnos, about which they wrote brilliantly in their book *The Sponge Divers*. The island of Kalymnos was where most sponge divers came from, and the book pays tribute to their hardiness as well as detailing the ghastly affects of 'the bends', which crippled so many of the male islanders who were engaged in the dangerous activity of diving for sponges.

Philip Ramp's 'On the *Flying Dolphin* to Aegina: An Elegy' is by contrast a poem by an American poet who has lived on the island since 1971, who now has Greek citizenship, who loves the place, but who, alert to history, especially contemporary history, is all too aware that any attempt to preserve Greece as a sort of timeless, comforting idyll is not merely sentimental, it is an absurd evasion of the often tawdry reality of the island as, for all its beauty, it now is.

On the Flying Dolphin *to Aegina*

An Elegy

Bucking along on the hydrofoil, the 'Flying Dolphin'
as it's called, feeling more like a virtual cowboy on
a real sea bull, I remembered how I used to slow waltz
my way home to my island on the old unhurried ferry –
usually the last one to drag itself out of an evening,
creaky and sluggish as the day had by then become,
and how I had stood out on the deck, watching earth
and sky as they bobbed about fashioning their equivocal
but no less certain response as to which was the master

of the evolving mind, stirring into the mix a convincing
star-thoughtful night, the ripples of wind from space
off the water, the last of the original conception that began
in their light, stark and dread-devised but not empty yet,
the essence of life as it spreads faced with the inexorable
deluminescence of even infinity, making unintelligible
but hauntingly familiar shapes, mingled and composite –
reflections of their endlessly reimagined surfaces?
Under such circumstances, it wasn't a stretch to imagine
the island coming into view as a rapid sketch, as rapidly
filling with substance, a form of monumental animation,
skilfully camouflaged by night-shadows, as mysterious as
the dark matter that shadows the universe, but still a
convincing simulation of how everything that has gone
into me here is really thinking of something else.
[. . .]
Things move much faster now. So I can come back later,
much later, reading in my seat, no deck to 'contemplate'
from, no place to smoke, nothing to drink, and so reading,
nearly level with the sea, glancing now and then through
the salt-crinkled plastic of the porthole as sudden bursts
of foam come sneaking up and leaping with dolphin playfulness . . .

Still in the light reflected from inside the cabin these drops
can seem almost frantic as they bead, filling the 'glass'
with their sinuous scrawl, like hurried messages sent out in
the dark in the hope of . . . making 'prophetic tracks across
the cloud-chamber of my mortality'? as I once noted to myself,
thinking of how I might have seen them, if I'd seen them,
when the ferry still plied this route, though of course they
were not in any real sense possible to then see, unless
the 'prophecy' is being fulfilled by what I now do see . . .

the image blurs, as my vision blurs from too much looking
out, no longer able to see tracks, messages and notes, in the
aimlessly restless water, and so no symmetry broken, space
and time can be fully regravitized to suit the theory of what
all things will mean when they are finally seen not for what
they are doing but for what they are . . . less than philosophy
more than . . . whatever that form of free association is that
aspires to poetry but satisfies itself with a metaphoric
vagueness of phrase: till the time, anyway, when that other
water, black and silver I imagine it, will, boiling, rise and
seep away whatever remnant of my consciousness may
still be intent on clearing the view, and being thus distanced
will find that what it had always suspected isn't yet true.

More likely the time is better spent reading a detective novel,
for in fact with the foreshortened vista there's little time
to indulge in any speculation as the island soon comes
surging through the water, dripping with its own lights
as if it too were out riding on the sea of night, or, more
appropriately to the time and ethos, was a casino cruise
ship, perhaps tethered for one night here, to fleece the
unsuspecting, to raise the stakes in the existence game . . .
anyway vaguely operatic in its ornament but given
to the bathos of vaudeville reviews, or grander gestures
flung out without a grand stage to hurl them from,
sweeping Wagnerian infinities reduced to the click
of finite wheels grinding fate into grains of bad luck . . .

the hard crack of the boat against the wake of a passing
ship makes the island tremble, and its light briefly
offers up an alternative map of the star-filled night
above, and in so doing a quite different reverie is
thereby jostled loose: the island not an island or a

ship but a galaxy all its own, one quite like ours but as
it trembles in the watery light I'm sure it has even less
time to endure the doom we're all racing toward,
and the enormous moon, under cover of my reverie
it would seem, has shaken free of the hills' embrace,
anyway, is not ours but its; more elaborate, a royal-red
seal on a document, an engraved guarantee that the
text it's beaming to all the quantum corners of night
is genuine, precious if only for that, and couched in phrases
that, though in essence alien, are so much like ours it
seems almost uncanny at first and ... then ... more natural
than any alternative I can think of: what one's been led,
after all, to expect of an *anthropic* universe, isn't it?

The hydrofoil deflates and wallows for a moment in the
foul trough the harbour has become and as it waits to dock
I reflect that meant to be or not this floundering may in
the near future feel normal: swamped by the thickening
effluent of our technological genius/malaise, reduced to
mere homunculi spinning our flagella in the heat-death
waste we have created in trying to create immortality, and
thus spawning a monstrous *ad hoc* disorder, an unconsciously
ironic imitation of the imagination that originally made
order out of chaos, closing the local loop in the circle ...
the aluminium 'gangplank' scrapes across the cement
and crashes down on the *Dolphin*'s 'wing': that's that.

The abrupt, snapped-off phrase with which the poem bumps to a
halt implies not merely the conclusion of an individual journey but,
however tempered by irony, a larger sense of ending.

　　Ramp's poem takes for granted that the reader will know
something of the meaning of dolphins in Greek myth and legend.

They feature as mysterious, emblematic visitors from the sea's rich depths, playful, joyous, but also of use: they carry shipwrecked humans to land, and they are appreciative of song. Hence, the importance of the story of the poet, Arion, and of his rescue from the sea. Arion was born at Methymna, on the north coast of Lesbos, and although the date of his birth is not known, he is said to have been a pupil of the poet Alcman, who flourished in the second half of the seventh century BC. He is also said to have spent years at the court of Periander, Tyrant of Corinth, and afterwards visited Italy, where he accumulated much wealth. He then decided to return to the island of his birth, but the sailors of the ship on which he sailed threw him overboard in order to share out his treasure among themselves. However, before sending him to his watery death they allowed him to sing one last song, a request which saved his life, because a dolphin, charmed by the song, carried him safely to land.

The mechanical *Dolphin* which brings Philip Ramp to an island can provide no guarantee of rescue from death. Indeed, with its plume of oily smoke, noise and remorseless 'frantic' haste to complete its journey, this dolphin seems almost a harbinger of death. But there are other dolphins still to be found in the Aegean, ones that Arion would recognise, and to which tribute is paid at the end of this anthology, though their numbers are diminishing and those that remain are under threat and not often to be seen, except in the waters that surround the wilder, less inhabited islands.

THE CRUEL SEA

As are all seas, the Aegean is associated with death and destruction as well as with new life. Aphrodite, born of the sperm generated by Uranus's genitals which Kronos cast into the sea after he had castrated him, emerged from the waves at Paphos, in Cyprus. Icarus, launched into the air above Crete with the aid of wings constructed for him by his father Daedalus, plunged to his death into the sea somewhere off the island now known as Ikaria. And then there are the sea battles, from Homer to the two World Wars. In between came the defeat of Xerxes' vast fleet off the island of Salamis, the Battle of Lepanto (1571), in which the combined navies of Spain, Genoa and Venice all but destroyed the Turkish fleet, and the various sea battles of the Greek War of Independence. Icarus's death becomes the unremarked event of Auden's great poem 'Musée des Beaux Arts', and is written about at length in Michael Ayrton's *The Testament of Daedalus*, where Icarus exults in his power as he flies above the sacred island of Delos:

> See the earth sparkles, glittering gives ground
> And rises gasping from the birth of day
> So that the lion hills that lift their round
> And bossy brows beneath the helmet heat
> Shake as the armoured morning leaps to greet
> Their ancient harness and their crests of clay . . . .
>
> Time has the scent of thyme, the dove starts up
> And claps her fluting wings against the vault
> So that with clapping clatter in the cup
> Of morning, Time is feathered as it turns:
> The minutes flicker and the morning burns
> To lie like jetsam in the rime of salt.

But then, his wings melted by the sun, Icarus falls to his watery death, where his voice, mingling with the varying sounds of the sea, utters a kind of non-Christian, non-Lycidas-like mantra of survival, one not so much focused on the self as on an unsubduable daring:

> No element divides the silences,
> The muffled sea robes this my tidal bed;
> The salt and fretted foams are now my skies,
> The air I breathe, unbreathing, is the sea
> That restless stirs beneath my restless head . . .
>
> Yet I am blind, who feared the shroud of dark
> And I am blackened ash who loved the light,
> Who sought to love the sea and still defies
> The deep sea darkness, holding to my love.
> What death is there for me who died in flight?

Ikaria is the setting for a far more recent death by drowning, the resonance of which is delicately alluded to by the poet Nadine Brummer.

End of Holiday

(Ikaria, 2002)

> Hands were nibbled by fish –
> shoals of minnows and sprats
> mobbed terrapins
>
> I fed in a freshwater inlet
> on a beach on Ikaria.
> Going there, our last day, we met
>
> Dave in blue T-shirt and jeans
> who stopped us to say,
> 'I've just seen a boy drown.'

He'd trained his binoculars on
Three youths swimming far out
When the wind got up and no one,

In their right mind, would risk
those white-capped waves.
He'd seen three boys going in,

diving from rocks into breakers
as if they were taking off
for manhood, the silly buggers,

and then there were two emerging
who flopped on to the sand;
a woman had started howling.

We turned back, went on to dine
at Costa's, ate mackerel and mullet,
drank still-fermenting wine,

watched small boats circling round,
bobbing and weaving like birds,
till the body was found.

Six hours on the ferry came late
and a priest in his tall hat
came out of the waiting crowd to meet

a silvery coffin that distracted the eye
from the ghost-light of stars
and the glimmer of lanterns marking

beautiful departures.
Dave travelled home by air,
economy class, left his binoculars

hanging over an airport chair.

But the majority of those whose lives are claimed by the Aegean are those who go to sea to work: sailors, fishermen, sponge-divers. Hence, for example, the anonymous 'Ballad of the North Wind', a dirge sung in commemoration of Greek sailors lost at sea, and well translated by George Dandoulakis.

Master North sent a message to all boats:
'Boats out at sea and all passing galleys,
cast anchor in harbour; for I'm going to blow hard,
cover vales and mountain peaks with snow,
and freeze all springs and fountains. And take note,
whichever boats I come across in the open sea,
I'll have them wrecked upon rocky land!'
No sooner had the boats heard his threat
than all made for harbour, except one!
Captain Andreas' galley still sails in the open.
'You do not scare me, Master North, however hard you blow!
My boat's made of walnut wood, and my oars of beech.
Its keel is of bronze and its mast of steel.
The sails are made of silk, fine silk from Prussia,
and its ropes from a fair lady's hair.
I've chosen the crew with care, each one a fine warrior
and a young sailor who can forecast the weather;
and whenever I set the boat's course,
nothing can make me change it!

'Now up the mid mast, my boy!
Check the wind and choose the time to sail.'
The young sailor climbed up with laughter,
but now comes down in tears.
'What did you see up there, my boy?'
'I saw the dim sky and bleeding stars;

I saw the thunderstorms break and flash;
the moon was lost to blackness; hailstones and lightnings
fell upon Attaleia's ridges.'

No sooner had the sailor finished
than a huge thunderstorm broke out
and the boat's rudder began to creak.
The sea foams and rages; the masts shake and splinter;
waves rise high; the boat shivers and quakes.
A blast of wind strikes her one side,
and a second blast strikes the other;
a third blast hits both sides
and breaks the hull to pieces;
masts and sails cover the sea
and palikars fill the waves.
Now the young sailor's body
floats forty miles away!

All mothers weep and console each other,
but there's nothing to console a young boy's mother!
She gathers some pebbles and stones, fills her apron
and runs down to the shore. There, she stands
and throws her stones at the sea,
scattering the pebbles on the waves:
'O sea, bitter sea, sea with bitter waves:
you've drowned my son, my only child!'
'It's not my fault, poor me,
nor are the waves to blame!
It's the shipbuilder's fault, who made his boat
too weak to withstand the wind's rage!
So, I'm losing my boats, my ornaments, so dear;
I'm losing my brave sailors, my fine singers!'

In his poem *To Axion Esti* ('Blessed is the'), his hymn of praise to Greece and of the struggle to restore light over the powers of darkness, Odysseus Elytis lists many of the popular names for winds that affect the Aegean, names used mainly by seamen. They include: Maistros, Levantos, Garbis, Pounentes, Zephyros, Graigos, Siroccos, Ostria, Tramountana, Meltemi. The last two are north winds, sometimes of destructive force. Small wonder Aeolus commanded Odysseus to keep tight hold of the leather bag in which the god had secured the winds that would blow the wanderer off course if they were set free. And guess what happened. Hence, Jen Hadfield's wild, exuberant 'Odysseus and the Sou'wester'.

> I caught and oxtered it like a rugby ball,
> a bloated bell of beating leather,
> and for weeks I nannied the bloody thing –
> on my lap, mending sails,
> in a papoose, to climb the rigging
> when the boys got steamed on Aeolian wine,
> I cuddled my squirming supper of winds –
> let no one spell me for a wink of sleep.
> From Aeolus to Malea was a waking dream.
> Fat kingcups wobbled like boxing gloves.
> With open eyes, I dreamt of home.
> I clicked my heels on the blinking squill,
> pillowed my skull on my second head,
> and the boys said
> > > > *oo*mpa-pa
>
> *oo*mpa-pa
> > > Rockabye Baby!
> > as I dandled us home
> > on the sweet vesper gale.

*   *   *

Now the low, brown island strains on tiptoes,
and fences are strung with trembling streamers,
and the sea's mad as milk.

And my cheeks are scored with milky tears.
And like a puffball breaks the bag of winds.

And there's the Sou'wester,
a rising loaf of shuffled feathers,
struggling from the haversack
like a furious swan.

It may be one such wind that knocks a sailor overboard in the seventh of the sequence of twenty poems, 'Holding the Sea', by Richard Berengarten.

The sea's fists lunged at him, collared him
and held him in a loose, careless embrace
until he numbed and swelled. Then the sea's
thorough fingers, examining and probing,
pulled him down into her primeval world.

As if with elegant fins and sails, he flew
among coral chambers and corridors
of rock, ascending and descending each
of their levels and spirals, until the sea's fingers
brushed and rolled him back on her briny beach.

In *The Sponge Divers,* their fine book about Kalymnos, from where sponge divers mostly came, Charmian Clift and George Johnston report the conversation of one such diver, Christos, and his account of the dangers he and his fellow divers constantly faced. The 'bends' was the chief menace, which often left strapping young men, proud of their physique and diving abilities, cripples for their entire lives, but there were others.

'Twenty-six years I've been going down,' Christos was saying, 'and there are some things you learn that have got the truth in them. I eat today because I won't eat tomorrow. Whether we dive at twenty-five metres or seventy-five, you don't catch me having anything in my belly until the day's work is over. A cigarette maybe, a sip of water, but nothing more than that. I remember once on board the old *Tasoula,* diving off Sollum, and it was so damned hot . . . the helmet made steam when it hit the water. You could hear it spitting, like putting a wet finger on a hot iron. And old Soklerides was sitting there next to me, waiting his turn to go down, and his lips all black and cracked and his tongue hanging out like a dog's, and just before the *colazaris* gave him the nod he called for a mug of water. I was going to say something to him but he was an older man than me and he'd been diving a good many years, but I thought to myself, 'You poor, silly bastard, that mug of water can be the death of you!' And sure enough, that's the way it was. There wasn't even a signal, not a touch on the rope, but the *colazaris* knew something was wrong by the slack feel of it. We hauled him up – by Jesus! what a weight it was – and he was dead by the time we got the helmet off. All full of blood the helmet was, where it had squirted out of his ears and nose and mouth, and his eyes rolled right back so you could only see the white. They were open but you could only see the white. It wasn't a deep dive either – forty metres maybe.

But the sea's cruelty can also be used as a metaphor for Greece's difficulties, both historic and contemporary. Hence, George Seferis's 'In the Manner of G. S.', whose closing lines run:

Meanwhile Greece goes on travelling, always travelling,
And if we see 'the Aegean flower with corpses'
It will be with those who tried to catch the big ship by
                                        swimming after it,
Those who got tired of waiting for the ships that cannot move,
The *Elsi*, the *Samothraki*, the *Amvrakikos*.
The ships hoot now that dusk falls on Piraeus,
Hoot and hoot, but no capstan moves,
No chain gleams wet in the vanishing light,
The captain stands like a stone in white and gold.

Wherever I travel Greece wounds me,
Curtains of mountains, archipelagos, naked granite.
They call the one ship that sails *Agonia 937*.

MS *Aulis*, waiting to sail
Summer 1937

The dating is essential to the poem's meaning. In early 1936, General Metaxas, the latest in a long line of army dictators, had come to power in Greece by overthrowing the government of the day and imposing his own mildly fascist form of rule. I have heard it said that the line 'Wherever I travel Greece wounds me', was sung on television by a 'trusty' of the Colonels who made up the villainously absurd Junta of 1967–74, and that her doing so sparked the student rising of 17 November 1973, which, although brutally suppressed, nevertheless marked the beginning of the end for the thugs who six years earlier had been set in place with the active connivance of the CIA. As Seferis put it in a commentary on his work quoted by Keeley and Sherrard in the Foreward to their edition of the *Collected Poems*: 'Men of inconstancy, of wanderings and of wars, though they differ and may change in terms of greatness and value … always move among the same monsters and the same longings.'

Nearly fifty years later, in 1985, David Gascoyne produced 'A Further Frontier', dedicated to Lawrence Durrell, a poem which bears the subtitle 'Viewed from Corfu':

> Seen across the leagues of amethystine calm,
> Two facing foreheads, one afforested,
> The other sparsely greened as with Greek-hay,
> An isthmus vista in between them hazed
> By distant fluorescent shimmering
> Of drowsy blended colours in which soot
> Suffuses violet, peach and ivory.
> Far to the East, a tranquil smoulder veils
> Some remote city old as Trebizond,
> Sated with myth and stunned by history,
> Where linger shades of despots, peasants, saints,
> Lost in oblivion's drifting dust. The end
> Of afternoon approaches, the tenth month
> Is almost here, further to obumbrate
> A land once white with dawn, the nearby shore
> Of North Helladic rock, whose dwellers owe
> Fealty alike to thoughts of men long dead.
> Night hovers like the question haunting all
> As to whether *eschatos* has not come.
> Unseen above hangs Saturn's fractured scythe.

In a note to the poem, Gascoyne says that 'A Further Frontier' was inspired 'by the view to be seen from the north of the isle of Corfu of the frontier dividing mainland Greece from Albania. Greek-hay is a variant of fenugreek ... The last line of the poem derives from the conclusion of Schiller's *Gruppe aus dem Tartarus* set as a *lied* by Schubert.' By *eschatos* Gascoyne means the final event in God's plan for the universe, in other words the end of the world. Looking from Corfu to Albania at a time when the intensifying of the Cold War seemed to threaten nuclear winter – 'oblivion's drifting dust' – he senses in the darkening mists of history and myth, and despite the beauty of sea and landscape, approaching apocalypse. Two years later my wife and I spent some weeks on Lesbos, as a result of which I wrote 'The Cemetery at Molivos', which strikes me now as a poem that revisits 'A Further Frontier', although at the time I wrote my poem I was quite unaware of Gascoyne's. (As far as I know, it was first published in Enitharmon's edition of his *Selected Poems*, 1994.)

The Cemetery at Molivos

The cemetery at Molivos is on a shelf of land sloping to sea:
you skirt the last, low farmhouse, its gnarled fig tree,
follow a track round pink-hazed laurel bushes,
past ambling, satyric goats, face heat that brushes
dry, spikey grass to gold, and suddenly you're there,
cypresses at each high white-walled corner
jetting like wax-dark flame into blue air.

On a still, sun-dazed morning we sauntered
among those comforting tombs. Beyond, the sky
was endless and so pure you said 'to lie
here would be good, our bones safe from it all.'
'All?'
     'The Bomb.'
                 I watched a caique haul
anchor to put out on an unmarked sea,
safe from clashing rocks or a god's fury,
and thought what other furies had left their mark
on this place of Arion, Sappho, Venetian, Turk . . .

But that's all past – and why not dream that here
our bones could settle down, that each new year
the sun alone would burst across its sky,
a goat's daft, randy bleat its one stark cry?

EMBARKATION FOR KYTHEREA

Most voyagers sail towards what they hope will be mystery, promise, the exotic and erotic hope of release from the dailiness of terrene existence. This is the burden of 'Sunday of the Aegean' by I. M. Panayotopoulos (1901–82):

> Sunday, day of the sun,
> walking like a dove on the washed stone wall,
> falling into our hands
> like apple blossom into a stream.
>
> Green islands filled with flaming blackberry brambles
> arrange themselves like anklets round your feet.
>
> Azure islands, worn about your neck
> as you sail on the billows,
> O Sunday of the Aegean!
>
> The seas are breathing citron and lemon
> – the maidens of Khios singing,
> the masts singing,
> the sails are singing
> and all things round about them blazing
> in the light of summer,
> the sun sunk in their brains.
>
> Soon the trireme of Paris will drift across our vision
> – and it will mount high
> toward the land of Troy.

With a reed pipe at their lips
let the unskilled shepherd boys stand
in the pasture land of Mount Ida
voicing the hymeneal song.

It is thus in all its body, shivering in the midst of summer,
and when it turns into a drop of dew,
that the Aegean remembers your passing feet,
that it remembers your beauty,
Helen!

(translated by Kimon Friar, adapted by the editor)

Buoyed up by such hopes, Watteau's courtiers embark for Kytherea (in modern Greek, Kithera), the southernmost of the Ionian islands and in ancient times dedicated to the worship of Aphrodite. Odysseus must have sailed past it towards Ithaka, but long before then, in the north Aegean, he had found and abandoned his own island paradise with the nymph Calypso. Pope's account is the finest of all English versions of the Fifth Book of the *Odyssey*, and though the great scholar Bentley's put-down – 'A very pretty piece of poetry, Mr Pope, but you must not call it Homer' – no doubt has its justice, it glances harmlessly off the description of Calypso's cave:

Large was the grot, in which the nymph he found
(The fair-hair'd nymph with ev'ry beauty crown'd),
She sate and sung; the rocks resound her lays:
The cave was brighten'd with a rising blaze:
Cedar and frankincense, an od'rous pile,
Flam'd on the hearth, and wide perfum'd the Isle;
While she with work and song the time divides,
And through the loom the golden shuttle guides.
Without the grot, a various sylvan scene

Appear'd around, and groves of living green:
Poplars and alders ever quiv'ring play'd,
And nodding cypress form'd a fragrant shade
On whose high branches, waving with the storm,
The birds of broadest wing their mansion form,
The chough, the sea-mew, the loquacious crow,
And scream aloft, and skim the deeps below.
Depending vines the shelving caverns screen,
With purple clusters blushing through the green.
Four limpid fountains from the clefts distil,
And ev'ry fountain pours a several rill,
In mazy windings wand'ring down the hill:
Where bloomy meads with vivid greens were crown'd,
And glowing violets threw odours round.

This description of an earthly paradise looks both backwards and forwards. Behind it is Milton's description of Eden in Book 4 of *Paradise Lost,* and in particular of the fountain that feeds 'many a rill' which mutate into 'crisped brooks/Rolling on orient pearl and sands of gold,/With mazy error'. And ahead lie the sacred river of Coleridge's 'Kubla Khan', 'five miles meandering with a mazy motion', and, I think, the volcanic cave that hides the freed Prometheus in Shelley's verse-drama *Prometheus Unbound* (1819). In a Prefatory Note to his revisiting of Aeschylus's tragedy, Shelley remarks that in preparation for writing his own poem, he has been rereading Milton, and although he completed *Prometheus Unbound* while sitting 'upon the mountainous ruins of the Baths of Caracalla, among the flowery glades, and thickets of odoriferous blossoming trees', this Mediterranean landscape belongs as much to island Greece as it does to mainland Italy, its ruins both summoning up remembrance of past glories and testifying to nature's healing power, its restorative beauty and fertility.

George Gömöri's 'Island in the Mediterranean', though not the island of Calypso, nevertheless takes on its magic properties as a place of erotic love, lived within time, the mother of beauty:

> Nothing is impossible on this island:
> Calypso might just be the name of a boat
> as much as a nymph. As for the sea,
> not wine-dark, it's more of a blue or green,
> gentian, or several shades of amethyst.
> But there it is, as the tale has it in H.,
> 'poplar and alder and fragrant cypress'
> and a monastery garden full of amphoras.
> Odysseus, under a vine-trellis,
> drinks wine; he does not brood on the shore.
> Seven days – not years – soon pass, no, run:
> an occasion for tears. By night the cave's
> redolent of parsley, no irises here –
> they've withered – just aloes and oleanders
> and endless fields of flowering lavender.
> The past grinds down the Trojan hecatomb
> and only the gods can see he'll make it home.
> Not for him immortality, for he of the gods' sweet
> idyll desires no part but, glad to have found love, he wave-like
> mounts and again comes to rest in Calypso's arms now,
>
> > the wanderer.

> (translated by Clive Wilmer)

Anita Sullivan's 'On Ikaria' evokes from a woman's point of view the coming of love, of erotic arousal and repletion:

> Under a pine tree
> on the side of a stony hill one eye

is enough for an afternoon, the sea
flings light up like wedding rice
beauty will save the world
eventually but I sit erect
like a single clover blossom in a meadow
waiting all day without patience
for its bee.

Alexander Hutchison's 'Epistle from Pevkos', addressed to the
Scots poet Gael Turnbull, is about embarkation and, indeed, arrival.
This is especially true of the first two of its twelve sections:

1

Gael, the bougainvillaea here sends greetings in the deepest
cloudy pink. Hibiscus too at the kitchen window – blatant
scarlet. Along the lanes nearby: acacia, almond, oleander,
fig. A full-blown date palm occupies the yard next door.
All round the house low grapevines trail a welcome.
Anna our kindly Pevkian *ya-ya* calls to water them first thing.

Behind the town the mountain ridge is grey and arid,
pecked and holed like tufa. At night in the starry dark
it looms at our back as banks of cloud.

2

Twice or thrice a day the steep down-shelving
blue *thalassa* laps us round. Staying afloat's no
bother here: the briny deep can raise us up
In temperatures equivalent to bliss.

Anyone would want to swim in this,
whether they could swim or no.

The point is that anyone coming from northern Europe is bound to be struck not just by the languorous heat but by the vivid, intense colours, blues, reds, yellows, the smells, at once delicate and earthy, pine-scent and dung, jasmine and rotting fruit, the sounds of island Greece, of ratchety, grinding cicadas, wind sifting through tamarisk. Profusion, ripeness, fullness. Hence, the following poem of Matt Simpson's:

Olives

Olives should come
from deep in the sea

plump eggs
of profoundest fish

limpet-fast
on fathom-drowned Aegean rocks

or profusions
of green and purple polyps

the swollen buds
of shimmying kelp

should bob
to the surface once a year

and there should be
a heady festival to grace

their scooping-up
olive-fishers singing

holdsful sloshing
back to harbour

in the lavender haze
of late afternoon

Why, it could be the lotos-land of Tennyson's shipwrecked travellers where

> . . . sweetened with the summer light,
> The full-juiced apple, waxing over-mellow,
> Drops in silent autumn night.
> All its allotted length of days,
> The flower ripens in its place,
> Ripens and fades, and falls, and hath no toil,
> Fast-rooted in the fruitful soil . . .

although Tennyson, never having been to Greece, had to guess what so beguiled Odysseus's men when they came to the land of the lotus-eaters and ate the flower that made them 'forgetful of their homeward way', so that they had to be brought back, reluctant and weeping, to the ships.

SNAPSHOTS AND POSTCARDS

It is difficult not to take an attractive photograph of a Greek island. All those blue skies melting into blue seas, the white fishing boats, some with grizzled fishermen in the stern, others with octopus draped over mast-lines and left to dry in the unremitting sun. Houses, piled like sugar cubes, seemingly on top of each other, doors and shutters painted blue as the sea, purple bougainvillea splashed across their frontages, steep, flagged steps up which a panniered mule labours while a grey-haired matriarch, all in black, sits side-saddle gazing at nothing. Clichés, of course, but saved from staleness by the sheer beauty of those primary colours, that vivid, unyielding light, the heat and, what no snapshot can provide, the scents: the fragrance of herbs and grasses that flourish in the fields each spring – basil, thyme, mint, oregano; the acrid-sweet summer smell of tall grasses so dried by the sun that they rattle in the merest breeze; the deep, warm scent of dungy earth. These are primal, as are the groves of olive trees with their impossibly gnarled, knobby trunks, leaves turning silvery-grey and glittering as light catches them, so that it's easy to imagine yourself surrounded by shoals of small fry, fallen impossibly into fields, or wandering among a forgotten treasury of long-discarded obols.

Here is Nadine Brummer's fine poem about such trees seen on the island of Samos.

Olive Trees

for Christopher Reid

Climbing uphill through short
contorted trees
I try to read their marks,
knots, nubs, scars, blebs, spurs –
the selfhood of trees
where wood wrestles with wood.
I love their convoluted writhing,
the way they clench something inside
that can't be expressed
though they let go of their fruits
when the nets are spread.
Sometimes you see one
almost bowed to the ground
holding on to, no, holding together
a remnant of wall
by muscle and roots
as if it might reach,
through soil that crumbles,
that dumbness, there
at the heart of things.

And here is Anita Sullivan, also absorbed in a scene in which the natural and human are blended in a manner that seems so ancient as to be ahistorical, although on this occasion the setting is the island of Ikaria.

Paradise

There's a pig in it, snuffling among the olive trees,
though I will not see her
from the warm rock by the river
since you can't turn around
inside an eternal moment
once it begins.

I was expecting bears to come down
through the woods, from the hill on my left
and cross the path in front of me
as I headed towards the river,
but today the path is strangely silent.

So I sit on the warm rock.
The crumbling terraces are covered with wild grass,
the old gardens held up by piles of ancient stones.
I see from all angles,
see water tumbling over stones in dappled shadows,
confuse shadows with silence, feel something
that's beyond happy, translates as mild nausea
of falling, taking off my wings, draping them
on top of the small wooden gate.

Sometimes a moment will expand and lengthen to take in a more comprehensive view, as it does in this poem by the contemporary Greek poet, Yannis Kontos.

Hydra

Struck by the museum's guns
our ship keeled over.
The captain, five or six seagulls and the girl
who embroidered mermaids on the sea
steady the vessel.
Stretch up, we're climbing high.
And so we landed on the island!
The island. With its white stones. Treeless.
Full of dolphins. Anchorless. Drifting
back and forth. Changing latitude all the time
to confuse those who use compasses.
The islands. The Aegean.

In the morning, the sea had come into our house.

The harbour at Hydra is indeed guarded by cannon, and to enter its narrow gap all ferries have to swing broadside on. Kontos's poem plays with the sea voyager's initial impression: of the guns, the rocky, treeless island stretching abruptly above the little port front, and it also plays seriously with the idea of Hydra as another floating island, one whose identity is withheld from those who try to measure it by hard-and-fast means. It is a hot island – there is no shade and the heat bangs back off the stones and bare rock – but the poem's last line deftly catches the early-morning delight in sea scent and pale, sub-aqueous light that floods in through open windows.

Later in the day, as the sun ratchets up its heat, so the cicadas ratchet up their noise. Matt Simpson, on the island of Leros, takes a poem snapshot of this phenomenon.

Cicadas

I'd like to get a word in edgeways,
here on the balcony beside
this feathery tamarisk
ablaze with sound.

I'd like to raise my glass of ouzo,
milky as semen, high
in the late afternoon, to you
and procreation.

That's all you sing of, you
and your jazzy legs! And yet
to catch you at it needs
a laser eye. Yes, there,

like a tiny flake of bark,
one of invisible thousands
filling branches
with high-voltage noise!

Hard to believe you don't migrate
from tree to tree. Our tamarisk's
become an abrupt silence
and in the pistachio orchard over the way

another tree is all a-fizz.
now suddenly you're back:

every single one of you
switched – presto – on again.

Trying to catch in words the sounds cicadas make is notoriously difficult. In his 'Poem from Tokyo', the Welsh poet John Davies says that 'cicadas/zipped and unzipped trees', for the Yugoslavian poet Ivan Lalic the sounds is that of a red-hot coal being plunged into cold water, Norman McCaig has the cricket (a smaller relation) 'scour his little pail', I myself have described the sound as reminiscent of water sloshing through gravel, and in his *tour de force* 'Tithonus', from *Horse Latitudes,* Paul Muldoon, trying to nail a sound that puzzles him, finds that it is

> Not again the day-old cheep of a smoke detector on the blink
>   in what used to be the root cellar
> but what turns out to be the two-thousand-year-old chirrp
>   of a grasshopper.

By evening the cicadas have packed it in. The night is reserved for the high whoop of Athene's owl or the silence in which the American poet Jack Gilbert nicely captures the thisness of living on a Greek island:

The Edge of the World

> I light the lamp and look at my watch.
> Four-thirty. Tap out my shoes
> because of the scorpions, and go out
> into the field. Such a sweet night.
> No moon, but urgent stars. Go back inside
> and make hot chocolate on my butane burner.
> I search around with the radio through
> the skirl of the Levant. 'Tea for Two'
> in German. Finally, Cleveland playing
> the Rams in rain. It makes me feel
> acutely here and everybody somewhere else.

But a little later the roosters begin their cries. There's a story that, standing on the Acropolis in the early hours one morning, a group of poets, among them Lawrence Durrell and George Seferis, indulged in the fancy that the first rooster's cry of day might alert other cocks to their duty so that, one by one, they would join in until the whole world was ringed by their cries. Impossible, of course. Wordsworth imagined the cuckoo's song 'Breaking the silence of the seas/Among the farthest Hebrides', but no bird song could cross the immensities of ocean in the southern hemisphere. In the northern one, though? Well, perhaps. And certainly the rooster's cry on a Greek island – that sound which at first, in Elizabeth Bishop's fine phrase, 'grates like a wet match' – insistently rises and swells until all over the island roosters are at their morning duty. This is the starting point for a poem I wrote from the island of Andros, which is dedicated to the two Greek friends with whom my wife and I so often share island holidays.

A Postcard from Andros

for Manos and Fotini

A six a.m. rooster's on morning call
and here come hills shaping up for day.

When I put my foot through water, fish
bicker round an inexplicable kouros.

Midday sun stirs deep, sweet scents,
though 'ochia' hide in fig trees, our friends warn,

those ash-grey branches
condominiums for small, ash-grey snakes.

'It's a rime-riche world,' I tell them, like those stacked
lion-mane terraces where goats browse, bells'

tink tink drying on valley air, or this pair
of bag-uddered cows who sashay past our hotel

at ouzo hour's pure floating of white –
doves about their towery, white-stoned cotes.

Later, through thyme-spiked
owl-whickery dark

we'll reach the earth's edge, hear
sea turn over in its moony sleep.

The American poet Charles Fishman also writes about 'Andros
Night', though he chooses to head towards the lights.

Darkness came up, so we walked
into town. An old woman had shown us
the short-cut: through the wood that opened
below the village, along the small turbulence
of the creek – just keep to the path and we'd be safe.
The night settled around us, but we found the road,
and the lights on the coast awoke.

Later, we met other travellers, ate with them
and drank. Simple food, good wine, and talk of home –
what could be sweeter? Someone – perhaps you, my friend –
bought another round. A bouzouki played in the distance
and the shore of the island swayed. Sweet fellowship
of the night breeze and the bottle! I think we sang
the anthem of lost brothers.

Then we headed back toward the village and the lights
of the town blew out. We walked slowly upwards,
talked of poetry and love. The stars circled above us.
But the secret path, this night, would remain a secret,
its entrance hidden in the Andros dark. What great poets
we would be, if we could drift between worlds: poet-
angels, whose words would have the brightness of comets.

But, this night, we were merely lost: the empty
white churches and their cobalt cupolas did not waken,
nor did the roadside shrines glisten as we stepped
through starlight. Bound to this earthly plane.
Here is where we would labour over our lines and here
we'd caress all we loved. We were lost in Andros night.
We circled upwards. The breeze of an old darkness chilled us.

A bit too long for a postcard perhaps, but the mixture of tongue-in-cheek awareness of how visitors fool themselves into believing that the place confers a special grace on them, together with an understandable desire to be lost in a dream of Andros night, will be familiar enough to all who for the first time step ashore on a Greek island.

For those familiar with the islands, there can be no such delusions. Here, to finish this section, is a masterly poem by the Greek–Australian poet Dimitris Tsaloumas.

Aubade for the Lady of Ships

On bastions torn off ragged night
shrill cockerel bugles declare
the day's intentions.

I lie alert
suspicious of my dreaming.

Yet peacock-proud the sun
spreads out a tail of majesty
above the Levant hills

shreds from holy vestments
of emperors and priests
ripple to my shore

and I see you walk into a light
made perfect in the dark.

Soon there'll be wings and voices
in the harbour, perhaps a wind
in the rigging of your ships.

This strange, beautiful poem, which at a casual glance seems almost like a quick-fading, phantasmagoric snapshot, doesn't have to be set on Leros, the island where Tsaloumas spends each summer. But the shreds of holy vestments of emperors and priests suggest that for the waking dreamer there can be no respite from the pressures of history and that history doesn't allow for an untroubled resting place. The wind in the rigging urges the need to fare forward.

BRIEF ENCOUNTERS

Many Greek islands still possess the visible evidence of their ancient histories. In *Ikaria, A Love Odyssey on a Greek Island,* her affectionate account of time spent on the island, Anita Sullivan has a chapter on Ikaria's bees and their hives.

> The bees are enormous. Among the hillside herbs in spring the droning is a constant thunder at the bottom of the air, so that if you did not see them, you would swear an odd new weather had set itself up in this place. The bee-sound is loud enough to drown out the sea a hundred feet below …

Ikarians began to use the modern, wood-built beehives – *kypseli* – in the late nineteenth-century. Before then, they had made use of stone hives, 'stone rectangles, each covered with a clay cylinder', which were clustered together in villages. The villages survive, but the bees have departed for the newer hives. As to the varieties of honey, these include two local specialities. One made from heather, which is not sweet, 'comes out looking like a beige bar of soap' and has to be melted before it can be put on toast, although an early-morning taster will make you 'feel full of energy for the rest of the day', Sullivan is told. The other is what the islanders euphemistically call 'pine honey'. An islander explains:

> It's made from a kind of worm-shit. The ubiquitous island pine trees have a parasite, a tiny worm-like creature, which eats the bitter bark … In March they emerge from the bark and the trees are covered with a white excretion from their bodies. This happens to be sweet, and the bees love it. They lick it, cover themselves with it, and turn it into 'pine honey'.

In this wryly reported encounter between a modern American and an islander, Rachel Hadas describes the visit she received from a gypsy on the island of Samos.

Samian Morning, 1971

The gypsy loomed in the open door of morning,
Bulky, unsmiling, her head wrapped in a scarf.
Her hand was out. She wanted something from me.

I don't remember whether I faced her fully.
Had I looked her straight in the eye and then beyond her,
I would have seen the Aegean like a frame.
If I had looked far enough over her right shoulder,
I would have seen Patmos lifting in a strip of light
from the horizon's lip. Over her left
shoulder I could have craned and seen Ionia.
But both of these radiant regions were blocked off
not only by the figure in the doorway.

Where had she come from? Behind the house was a field.
Beyond the square green field – it was a wheatfield –
were a bent fig tree and a low stone wall
and a whitewashed hut like a gatehouse. Behind the wall
a road wound north away from the coast to the village.
She could have just walked up Poseidon Street
to ours, the last house in the row. But I think
she came round from the side, the back, the north.
I used to think the wind blew straight from Russia.
Turkey was left, the east,
and right and west was the great granite mountain.

My stinginess and resentment balanced by shame,

I gave the gypsy something I remember
probably only because she scowled and reproached me.
Whether she came back a second time
to try again, another woman with her,
is wavering conjecture. But I see all right
the thing I gave her: bright yellow, cashmere,
still with its Saks Fifth Avenue label,
a sweater someone had given me, no doubt,
for the same reason I tried to palm it off
on the gypsy, who rejected it with scorn.
The sweater was marred. A stain like a port-wine birthmark
splotched the front. Who would wear such a thing?
Not I. Not she. I recall the botched transaction
but have to supply the shining of the sea,
brilliant backdrop to the piebald life
I must have turned back to after the gypsy, grumbling,
took herself away from the open door,
though I do not know if I turned to it with relief.

Brief encounters have to try to span cultural divides that may
prove too wide and deep for the bridge to hold. Misunderstandings
can produce distrust. An older way of life confronts and is offended
by the assumptions of modern Western capitalism, no matter how
well intentioned. Peasants are simple and quaint. They aren't
complicated like us. They have different attitudes to time and
money. Believe it if you will.

But misunderstandings can also be comic. The following is my
versification of an encounter reported to me by Gerald Thompson, a
classical scholar who for the past twenty years has made his home
on the island of Aegina.

Faith and Reason: An Aeginetan Dialogue

Near the top of that boulder-clogged
Pine-dark path, you said, a scold
Nun appeared to thwart your progress.
'What are you doing here and why?'
'Searching, Sister. I've been told

Of pure views not far ahead.'
'Such foolishness! And don't you know
You risk your life from vicious snakes
Clustered across this path you tread?
Go back at once to your ways below.'

'Sister, I have a walking stick!'
'What then?' Time for the *coup de grâce*.
'The wood was cut on Holy Mountain,
Sister!'
      A winning smile. 'And do you
Think our snakes know that, you ass?'

Pre-Christian, classical Greece survives most powerfully, perhaps, on the island of Delos, where as visitors are not permitted to stay their encounter with its architectural remains is necessarily brief. Pindar gives an account of the island's sacred origins.

Ode to Delos

Hail to you, god-made island dearly loved
by the children of dazzling-plaited Leto:
daughter of the sea, unmoving miracle
in the vastness of the earth, Delos
to mortals, to Olympian gods

a bright, distant star of the blue world.
Shifted about in times past
by waves and contrary winds,
when the Titans' daughter
laboured ashore in her last
child-bearing convulsions,
four iron-girthed pillars rose
from the unplumbable deeps to hold
this rock-island on their capitals;
and here the goddess, finally at rest, gazed
tenderly at her new-born twins.

Pindar was born about 520 BC and died some eighty years later. Famous during his lifetime, Pindar's posthumous reputation was sufficiently secure for Alexander to order that his house be spared during the sacking of Thebes in 355 BC. This short ode deals with matter treated by Hesiod in the *Theogony* (*c.* 800 BC), his genealogy of the gods. Leto was the daughter of the Titan gods Coeus and Phoebe. Lusted after by Zeus, she was impregnated by him, but because of Hera's jealous anger found that no land would receive her when the time approached for her to give birth. She eventually found refuge on Ortygia, a floating island, which Poseidon at once secured to the sea floor. There, on the island afterwards called Delos, she gave birth to Artemis and Apollo. Delos means 'which has come to light from', and this name underscores the poem's movement in its meaning of a journey, a crossing, from chaos to serenity and stability.

Given the uncertainty of map-making in ancient times, it is scarcely surprising that islands were often thought to wander, to float sponge-like rather than be attached to the sea-bed, but Delos has a special place in Greek myth and history as a sacred island. Hence, the following poem by C. A. Trypanis.

Delos

(Temple of Isis)

Seistrum and the situla of stone,
Trailing vanities of Isis ... the wind ...
Hard silence, locking the lion's jaws,
Gaping at a pond
Where once the withered darkness flashed in light.
Line answers line of stone, dead on a grassless world.

And the near masks of blue, dolphins
Curling round angry tridents,
Swim into a gagged marble floor.
Cool atria now,
The empty skulls of slaves
Licked white with time,
Bronze hoops of lizards
Clinging to the theatre steps, the rock,
Look down upon the beach,
Nile-green the water too clear to see the depth.
Trailing vanities of Isis ... the wind ...
Seistrum and the situla of stone.

Trypanis (1909–93) was for many years Professor of Byzantine and
Modern Greek at Oxford, a scholar and a poet who published
several collections of poetry in English. This account of Delos takes
in the ruins of the famous Lion Terrace, the House of the Masks and
the House of the Dolphins, and of the theatre, with seating for some
five thousand spectators. In 'Trailing vanities of Isis', Trypanis is
presumably wanting to assimilate the ancient Egyptian goddess of
fertility with Leto, and it is of course true that the gods of the two
cultures do ghost each other, though I have to say that when I

visited the island there was nothing Nile-green about the colour of the sea surrounding it. 'Seistrum' and 'situla of stone' (*situla* means a bucket) refer to volcanic activity that produced the granite by means of which the island is anchored to the sea-bottom.

An altogether earthier brief encounter is provided by Chris Hardy, although Artemis is invoked.

Just in Case

> She was spitting into her goggles
> and removing her top;
> not pleased to see me
> coming over the rocks
> she sat up and covered herself
> with her knees.
> I was polite in response to her
> vexed morning greeting.
>
> I saw her black rump in the foam
> and moved my gear over.
> Later I cut my finger
> and as the drops detonated
> small red bombs in the sea
> I dedicated some to Artemis
> just in case.

For as Actaeon found, his stumbling upon the naked Artemis, innocent though he was of bad intent, did him no good. The goddess's punishment was to turn him into a deer who was then chased, brought down and killed by his own hounds. A beach-sign my wife and I came upon in 1985 somewhere in southern Crete warned, *The Nudish is Forbidding.* It is indeed.

ISLAND LOVE

There are several islands associated with love: love achieved, love denied, love as the wrecker of lives, love as redemption. Crete, for example. Here, according to one of the most powerful Greek myths, Pasiphae's unnatural love for a bull, instilled in her by Poseidon, who thus avenged himself on her husband, King Minos, for refusing to sacrifice the bull to the sea god, led to the birth of the Minotaur. Minos then demanded that Athens send a yearly tribute of seven young men and seven young women for the Minotaur to devour. Theseus, the son of King Aegeus of Athens, volunteered to accompany one such tribute and to kill the Minotaur. Ariadne, Minos's daughter, fell in love with him and gave him the thread by means of which he would be able to find his way out of the labyrinth in the deep heart of which the Minotaur was immured. Once Theseus had killed the beast and made good his escape, the pair sailed to Naxos where, callously, Theseus abandoned her. She later married Dionysus while Theseus, back in Athens, took Phaedre as his wife. There is inevitably much literature dealing with this sequence of tragic events; there is music, too, including opera; but, odd as it may seem, there are no poems of suitable length or sufficient interest to be included in the present anthology. I couldn't, however, ignore Alan Dixon's tart, ribald account of a latter-day Poseidon making the kind of claims for Greek manhood that come naturally to a culture where the gods commit rape as of right, and, as the Greek joke has it, Jesus must be Greek because every Greek mother believes her son to be God, a belief every son entirely shares.

At the Poseidon

Looking for trouble
to make something to say
for the long hot day,
sand, bodies and sea
and brown breast wobble,
he strode to the middle
– in a pause in the music
and clinking of glasses –
of the crowded taverna
where no foreign female
has failed with the boys,
and shouted, 'Greek men
are the best in the world!'
The cheering was loud;
they raised their glasses
(so fond of the English)
observed by a frowning
Byzantine nereid
and brought him a bottle,
and brought him two,
and said it was true.

The shipwrecked Odysseus gave early proof of the validity of this claim. He didn't need to 'club women with sex', in Philip Larkin's phrase, they all reliably fell for him. Among them was Nausicaa, perhaps the most charming of the many women in the wily one's life. In his biography of James Joyce, Richard Ellman notes that at the time Joyce was writing the Nausicaa section of *Ulysses* (in which ageing Leopold Bloom ogles from a distance the young Gertie McDowell), Joyce himself was engaged in a romantic affair with a young Swiss woman, Marthe Fleischmann, whom Ellmann designates as the inspiration behind a short poem of 1918, 'Bahnhofstrasse'.

> The eyes that mock me sign the way
> Whereto I pass at eve of day.
>
> Grey way whose violet signals are
> The trysting and the twining star.
>
> Ah star of evil! Star of pain!
> Highhearted youth comes not again
>
> Nor old heart's wisdom yet to know
> The signs that mock me as I go.

The Nausicaa episode in *Ulysses* very nearly resulted in a prison sentence for the American publishers of the *Little Review*, where the section first appeared. It was, the judges at the trial found, obscene, and the two editors were each fined fifty dollars. Goodness only knows what punishment Homer would have incurred had he been arraigned before the same judges and called on to justify the shipwrecked Odysseus' glad discovery of the 'white-armed' daughter of King Alcinous, playing with her maids on the sea-shore where he lay naked, salt-grimed and exhausted. A. E. Stallings's mordant 'The Wife of the Man of Many Wiles' makes for a sceptical response to Odysseus' tale.

> Believe what you want to. Believe that I wove,
> If you wish, twenty years and waited, while you
> Were knee-deep in blood, hip-deep in goddesses.
>
> I've not much to show for twenty years' weaving –
> I have but one half-finished cloth at the loom.
> Perhaps it's the lengthy, meticulous grieving.

Explain how you want to. Believe I unravelled
At night what I stitched in the slow siesta,
How I kept them all waiting for me to finish,

The suitors, you call them. Believe what you want to.
Believe that they waited for me to finish,
Believe I beguiled them with nightly un-doings.

Believe what you want to. That they never touched me.
Believe your own stories, as you would have me do,
How you only survived by the wise infidelities.

Believe that each day you wrote me a letter
That never arrived. Kill all the damn suitors
If you think it will make you feel better.

But lovers apart can feel an erotic charge that survives physical distance, and time and space. Hence David Mason's 'Acrostic from Aegina':

Anemones you brought back from the path
Nod in a glass beside our rumpled bed.
Now you are far away. In the aftermath
Even these flowers arouse my sleepy head.

Love, when I think of the ready look in your eyes,
Erotas that would make these stone walls blush
Nerves me to write away the morning's hush.
Nadir of longing, and the red anemones
Over the lucent rims – my poor designs,
X-rated praise I've hidden between these lines.

And from the same island, as I happen to know, comes Michael Murphy's 'Morning Song':

Heat-struck, I lie awake,
imagining a body where there's none:
you, your heavy limbs at rest
beside me in our Welsh-pine bed
back home, and almost catch
the sound your breathing makes,
withdrawing, an ocean to the north.

Here, behind the old town,
a scooter gears up past the cypresses,
hot from a moonlit assignation.
Stars over the cemetery wall,
silent breakages of fire,
go down in the restless sky.
Bougainvillaea rehearses its torch song.

An hour from now
and the sun will start to climb
inch by slow inch
through the resinous pine,
fishing boats strung out across the bay
will rewind their nets
and I'll replay the words

you slipped into my case
I'll be dreaming of you
when you read this.
So, for now, let silence alone
make inroads into the night,
sifting the world for a sound
I can hold, as a shell, to my ear,

permitting each rigorous thing –
in itself – the soughing tide,
wind in the trees –
to arrange themselves as bluntly as
light reorders scattered sheets,
the precise blurring the matter-of-
fact: dawn and its homesick ghosts.

The setting of Murphy's poem is the little fishing village of Faros. Up in the middle of the island is the famous Palaiochora, the mediaeval capital, now mostly ruins, although as the island's historian, Gerald Thompson, writes in his *Walking Guide to Aegina*, despite the fact that the fort 'which once crowned the hilltop and . . . countless humble dwellings that clustered the winding streets, have long since crumbled . . . there survive some twenty-six chapels, many containing fine murals'. This site forms the *mise en scène* for David Constantine's beautiful, candidly erotic poem 'Honey from Palaiochora'.

It is hard to make out where Palaiochora is
        From here. You have to look up, higher up
Than you'd ever think there could have been a town, and find
        The upright that is not a wavy cypress tree
And that's the tower, still standing, lifted like a minestack,
        A pale sign. The rest is above and below
On ledges but even after you've been up there,
        Even with the sun on it and though you find
The Venetian belfry that has stood through earthquakes,
        Still hard to believe from here. On the island
In spring being in or out of the sun is black and white:
        You huddle, out; but in, you open up.

When we got down from finding Palaiochora,
    Carrying our heavy honey in a jar,
We made tea in a glass with a wheel of lemon in,
    Golden, and dug at the honey there and then,
Dripping it on broken bread with spoons. The sun rode down
    The line of the hill of Palaiochora
Full in on us. We slid the windows wide, we stripped,
    Every stitch off both of us. I took
The lingering honey and lemon off his tongue
    And he had his hand and the sun together
Between my legs, idling, the way I wanted it,
    Slowly, slowly, so that they gave me time

For all the roofless house of Palaiochora,
    Gone in now under the lee of the sun, back
Into the hill with all their clever paths and steps,
    To appear behind my eyes: flowers, flowers,
White irises and asphodel, poppies and drifts
    And flounces of purple vetch where people slept
And where they cooked and talked and over their wells and walls
    From level to level through their workplaces,
Terrace into terrace ushering through flowers and
    Everyone long since gone, centuries gone,
Except in the unroofed chapels under the sun
    Where it came and went and they were warm or cold

Only the fresco angels, they had stayed, they looked
    Ghostly in the day, ghostly in the flowers,
Being made for the dark and to come out glowing
    Under a roof with candles and now revealed
And fading day by day in the visiting sun:
    Angels blessing, angels announcing, but with

Faces of the boy or girl you would wish to have,
   Earthly, pleased, lifted, and showing a pale palm
For a sign where we found them, tall as adolescents,
   In the irises and the purple. Then I
Was in shadow, his, his hot shade, and felt for the sun
   Down the line of his back and as though he were

The sun I pulled him in, in, to ensure in me
   Before the lingering angels faded
Some seed of the flowers of Palaiochora
   Heaped in the standing frames of empty homes
Like quilts and linen, to have them body and soul
   Before the message and the blessing failed
In me while he was doubled by the sun I widened
   Where he reached and gave and met. Then waking,
Opening real eyes on a room replete with sun,
   Sun held us above black cypress candles,
I saw our jar of honey. It was lit from in,
   From in itself. I saw that first. It shone.

These poets have very different experiences of Greece. Alan Dixon and Michael Murphy (1965–2009) are English poets who would probably class themselves as casual visitors. A. E. Stallings is an American poet, married to a Greek husband, whose home is in Athens. David Mason (American) and David Constantine (English) have spent extended periods on the island of Aegina and have travelled elsewhere in Greece. All, however, pay tribute to the power of *erotas*. Erotic love is very different from Dame Kind (love of nature) and Agape (heavenly love). W. H. Auden, who made the distinctions between these three kinds of love, observed in his essay 'The Greeks and Us' that the ancient Greeks did not possess our modern, romantic conception that erotic love can ennoble, can indeed make a man or woman hero-like. There are two kinds of attitude to sexual love to be found in ancient Greek poetry, Auden claims in *Forewords and Afterwords*. 'There are lyrics of the serenade type – the "In delay there lies no plenty, then come and kiss me sweet-and-twenty" kind of thing, expressing a simple, good-tempered and unserious sensuality;' and, 'There are also, as in the poems of Sappho or the story of Jason and Medea, descriptions of serious and violent sexual passion.' The latter, he points out, 'is not regarded as something to be proud of but as a disaster, the work of merciless Aphrodite, a dreadful madness which makes one lose one's friends ...'

Modern literature is scarcely short of stories about disastrous love affairs, ones that feel as though they must be the work of merciless Aphrodite. But Auden is also guilty, I think, of unfairly representing Sappho's poetry. She *may* have committed suicide over an unhappy love affair and the object of her affection *may* have been a woman, but we don't know for sure. As the best modern commentators on her poetry have observed, it is almost certainly wrong to read the surviving fragments – some two hundred of them – as unabashed autobiography. All we can be certain of is that she lived in the city of Mytelene on Lesbos around 600 BC. In her splendid work *Classical Women Poets* (Bloodaxe, 1996), Josephine Balmer reports another modern authority, Joan DeJean, as saying that Sappho's poetry 'relegates men to a peripheral role, and is concerned almost exclusively with women – their family relationships, their religious festivals and female deities, particularly Aphrodite, and, most of all, their intense emotional relationships'. And, to paraphrase a line from Auden's poem 'Dover', some of these relationships are happy. At all events, the fragments we have don't all present love as a disaster. Undeniably, love may be a form of madness – but it is a sweet madness, a sweet disorder.

> Love shook my heart
> like the wind on the mountain
> rushing over the oak trees
>
> *
>
> Love makes me tremble yet again
> Sapping all the strength from my limbs

And here is a sizeable fragment about sexual desire and its torments:

> It seems to me that man is equal to the gods,
> that is, whoever sits opposite you
> and, drawing nearer, savours, as you speak,
> the sweetness of your voice
>
> and the thrill of your laugh, which have so stirred the heart
> in my own breast that whenever I catch
> sight of you, even if for a moment,
> then my voice deserts me
>
> and my tongue is struck silent, a delicate fire
> suddenly races underneath my skin,
> my eyes see nothing, my ears whistle like
> the whirling of a top
>
> and sweat pours down me and a trembling creeps over
> my whole body. I am greener than grass,
> at such times, I seem to be no more than
> a step away from death;
>
> but all can be endured since even a pauper ...

Even a pauper can what? Gaze on the beloved, I suppose, as a cat may look at a king. (Or queen.)

But love does not have to be storm, wind and fire:

> On a soft cushion I will soothe my tired body
>
> *
>
> [from our love]
> I want neither the sweetness of honey
> Nor the sting of the bees
>
> *
>
> I do not have a spiteful temper but a tender heart
>
> *
>
> May you sleep on the breast
> Of your tender companion

All these examples are taken from Balmer's outstandingly good *Sappho: Poems & Fragments*. And I have taken from her equally excellent *Classical Women Poets* the following poem, 'The Distaff' by Erinna, who, Balmer says, lived *c.* 350 BC 'in the region of Rhodes, or possibly on the island of Tenos, and died, according to ancient tradition, at the age of nineteen'.

>   . . . and those games, Baucis, remember?
> twin white horses, four frenzied feet – and one tortoise
> to your hare: 'Caught you,' I cried. 'You're Mrs Tortoise now.'
> But when your turn came to catch the catcher
> you raced on far beyond us, out from the great shell
> of our smoke-filled yard . . .
>   Baucis, these tears are your embers
> and my memorial, traces glowing in my heart,
> now all that we once shared has turned to ash . . .
>   . . . as girls

we played weddings with our dolls, brides in our soft beds,
or sometimes I was mother allotting dawn wool
to the women, calling for you to help spin out
the thread . . .

      . . . and our terror (remember?) of Mormo
the monster . . . big ears, and tongue, forever flapping,
her frenzy on all fours and changing shapes – a trap
for girls who lost their way . . .

          . . . But when you set sail
for a man's bed, Baucis, you let it slip away,
forgot the lessons you had learnt from your 'mother'
in those far-off days – no, never forgot; that thief
Desire stole all memory away . . .

          . . . My lost friend,
here is my lament: I can't bear that dark death-bed,
can't bring myself to step outside my door; won't look
on your stone face, won't cry or cut my hair for shame . . .
but Baucis, this crimson grief

          is tearing me in two . . .

One of the finest of contemporary Greek poets, Katerina Anghelaki-Rooke, who owns a house on the island of Aegina where she spends much time, has written with rare distinction about love and, for that matter, lust. She is the author of a wonderful poem, 'The Other Penelope', about trying to abandon the inevitable pains of love, in which Odysseus's wife becomes a potent symbol for all the contradictory feelings which love arouses.

The Other Penelope

Penelope emerges from the olive trees
her hair more or less tidy
her dress from the neighbourhood market
navy blue with white flowers.
She tells us it wasn't obsession
with the idea of 'Odysseus'
that pressed her to let the suitors
wait for years in the forecourts
of her body's secret habits.
There in the island's palace –
with the fake horizons
of a saccharine love
and only the bird in the window
comprehending the infinite –
she had painted with nature's colours
the portrait of love.
Seated, one leg crossed over the other,
holding a cup of coffee
up early, a little grumpy, smiling a little
he emerges warm from the down of sleep.
His shadow on the wall:
trace of a piece of furniture just taken away

blood of an ancient murder
a lone performance of Karaghiozi *
on the screen, pain always behind him.
Love and pain indivisible
like the pail and the child
on the sandy beach
the ah! And a crystal glass that slipped from one's hand
the green fly and the slaughtered animal
the soil and the shovel
the naked body and the single sheet in July.

And Penelope who now hears
the evocative music of fear
the cymbals of resignation
the sweet song of a quiet day
without sudden changes of weather and tone
the complex chords
of an infinite gratitude
for what did not happen, was not said, cannot be uttered
now signals no, no, no more loving
no more words and whispers
caresses and bites
small cries in the darkness
scent of flesh that burns in the light.
Pain was the most exquisite suitor
and she slammed the door on him.

(translated by Edmund and Mary Keeley)

---

* Karaghiozi. Shadow-puppet theatre introduced to Greece from Turkey.
Karaghiozis himself is an anti-hero, who uses his native wit to discomfort
and humiliate authority figures.

To end this section, here is another poem of Anghelaki-Rooke's, in which the woman narrator links love and death with an especially violent image. This is not so much Judith, entangled in the snare she set for Holofernes, as any woman suddenly aware that sexual love is animalistic quite as much as it is human.

Heat

In the heat of Greece
our sternums pressed together
spurted water.
I drank your sweat
along with your kisses
your sigh
in the shade of the shutters.
There as the violent afternoon
came on, you too were ablaze
with your tangled hair
your divine lashes
your laughter refracted
through the salty prisms of passion.
In the sizzling heat
in the total stillness –
the only shadow above us
black as destiny –
the outline of our existence
an equation of insects.
August festered
like an open sore
while relentless cicadas
echoed the poet's
closing lines.

Not a breath of air . . . .
The pedantic fly that defiles everything
sits on your cock
drinking your sap.
The water-melon man
passes with his megaphone.
   The afternoon
   falls at my feet
   like a severed head.

          (translated by Katerina Anghelaki-Rooke
                and Jackie Willcox)

ISLAND WORK

Among younger Greek poets whom Seferis encouraged was Dimitris
Tsaloumas, to whom he had been introduced through the good
offices of Lawrence Durrell. Soon after the end of the Second World
War, Durrell was going about the Aegean in preparation for writing
his book on the islands. Forced by adverse weather conditions to
spend some days on the island of Leros, which he detested, he met
the young Tsaloumas, recognised his talent, and recommended him
to Seferis. But Tsaloumas, who had worked for the Greek Resistance
during the war years, was a marked man. In 1952, he was forced to
leave his homeland, emigrated to Australia, and for over twenty
years was unable to return to Greece. When he did, it prompted a
series of magnificent poems in which island landscape, history and
social observation are braided together in complex celebration. As
here, in 'The Threshing-Floor':

> Down the slope of the declining year
> in light of resined wine and crystal glass
>
> I reached, not far above the setting sun,
> a threshing-floor and a humble house
>
> in shuttered loneliness. This is, I thought,
> how bread begins, and I sat on a stone
>
> to watch the blindfold horse that wound
> about a cruel spool the unending thread
>
> of its darkness. Then night fell and lights
> came on in the house, and sounds of lute

and festive talk. Angels with pitchers
came out laughing on the porch.

Their sandals creaked with untouchedness.
And how lovely their faces, the ikon folds

of their silks. My supper was blessed.
Yet it was wrong that in the sowing season

there should be harvesting. And my eyes
grew big with tears for the angels' horse

dark-bound in circles of racking memory
of his paddock in heaven. There must be help,

I cried. And I shook the carob-tree. And all
my brine-burnt fields grew lush with clover
knee-deep, with tall-stalked barley heads.
Cartloads of apples rolled down the hill
beneath my window. And I was comforted.
The threshing-floor below was full of moon.

Three girls I loved, hems stitched to slender
waists, black kerchiefs chin-fast, hummed low,

pitchforking moondust into the air. A wind
and a cypress moaned gently all night.

(*The Barge*, 1993)

To adapt Auden, August for the tourists and their favourite
islands, maybe, but as 'The Threshing Floor' reveals, islands are for
their inhabitants places of work. Richard Berengarten has a series of
poems which celebrate such work.

for Anastassis Vistonitis

Outside the café underneath the plane tree
the old sailors play backgammon.
Little they know or care about pasts or futures
who once chugged out past overhanging islands
and caught shoalsful of fish in their long nets.

Islands reached stony fingers out to grab them.
Hidden rocks and reefs sharpened their nails.
Waves grew claws to slash at them and snatch them.
Darkness itself unleashed invisible talons
and now they sit outside the café like ordinary men.

* * *

The young wives toil uphill ferrying water
and by the well the old ones knit and sew.
They are reeling in the ships far out at sea,
darning and mending aftermaths of wrecks,
snipping and bordering frayed hems of lives.

Even the strengths and directions of winds
and patterns of eruptions on ocean floors
get stitched by their gnarled fingers
and what they do they do
scarcely noticing the effects they achieve.

Modern Greek poets tend not to write about the world of work,
from which, to speak plainly, they are for the most part separated by
cultural expectations. Samuel Butler famously thought Homer must
have been a woman because, he argued, whoever composed the *Iliad*
and the *Odyssey* was more familiar with details of domestic labour –
cooking and sewing – than any man could be expected to be. But,

truth to tell, we learn very little about the details of Penelope's work. Towards the end, she reveals only to the returned Odysseus, whom she does not yet know to be her husband, that 'I set up a great web on my loom here and started weaving a large and delicate robe, saying to my suitors, "I should be grateful to you young lords, who are courting me now that King Odysseus is dead, if you could restrain your ardour for my hand till I have done this work, so that the threads I have spun may not be altogether wasted. It is a winding-sheet for Lord Laertes" ' (E. V. Rieu's Penguin version). But we are told nothing of the material out of which the robe is fashioned, nor of its design.

But then Greek poets say little about work more traditionally associated with men: carpentering, building, farming, fishing. Even Kavvadias is thin on the details of the working life of cargo boats. But a poem by S. Paschalis, 'The Farmhouse', rather beautifully provides a Hardy-like sense of 'presences', of the rural tradition.

> Living here's like crouching
> in an old, hollow chestnut tree.
> (Winter weathers have barked and notched its stone.)
>
> It's built country-style yet the
> furnishings are all city stuff:
> art-deco, art-nouveau and bric-a-brac
> saved from some sea-wandering past:
> this oak chest stuck with a lamp,
> its tacky opal base flecked red-gold.
>
> Here, it's autumn all year round, light
> beyond barred windows filtered
> by dark-green shutters, and only a few
> thin wisps of candle flame to reach the pomegranate
> from a door opening on to the hall's stone floor,
> its blotched, unsilvered mirror.

A house *sans* human ghosts:
its whiskery store rooms, jars,
tea-chests and olive-press
hunker in the dark.

But sometimes
in this place of job-lot styles
shadows from surrounding
olive groves lean on carved seats,
sofas, cluttered tables –

What stirs within its roofed walls
when under midday light
the trees sulk without reason?

It is therefore usually left to visitors to observe the work of
islanders, themselves sometimes short-stay, itinerant workers, as is
the subject of Matt Simpson's 'Scottish Waiter Bringing Squid'.

That last evening in Ayia Marina, before I left the island,
was filled with relishable things: warm night-air, Aegean lapping,
old mill paddling its feet in the bay, Byzantine castle
floodlit on the hill, the aniseed kick of ouzo, charcoal bite
of octopus grilled, bright conversations, a generous moon –

But most the waiter's quickly-rumbled suspect Greek,
his fervent *explication de texte,* then back to our table bringing squid
and bowing to you, Dimitris, with: 'The owner tells me you're
a celebrated poet . . . I write wee bits myself . . . '

Memorable is memorable and this was a night of satisfactions
worth some liberality. So, Scottish rhymster, here's to you
for the calamari and ouzo, and for adding zest to a bonny night
with the solemnity and swagger of your god-damn-awful verse.

(The island was Leros, the poet Dimitris Tsaloumas,
the poem is from *Getting There.*)

Preparing food is part of the *mise en scène* of the American poet
Michael Waters's poem 'Parthenopi', set on the island of Ios.

Once we beheld the brilliance of our estate
reflected in the haloed serenity of the girl
who prepared the basketful of cucumbers for salad,
slicing each nub into watery wheels,
columns of coins in the egg-white bowl.
Then she'd lift each miniature transparency
as she'd seen the priest flourish the Host,
thumb the serrated blade
to nick the green, then twist her wrist
to peel back the dust-plumed skin, the rubbery shavings
heaping a wild garden, unspoiled Eden, on the wooden counter.
Again and again she consecrated each wafer.
We basked in her patience, that rapt transportation,
her bell-shaped, narrowing eyelids as she spun
one papery sun, then the next, her perfect happiness,
smoke from the blackened grillwork wreathing her hair,
the fat of the slaughtered lamb hissing on the fire.
Her name – we'd asked the waiter – was Parthenopi, 'little virgin'.
We were still a couple then, our summer's lazy
task to gather anecdotes towards one future,
each shared and touching particular
to be recited over baked brie and chilled chardonnay
in the grasp of some furious, if distant, winter.
'Parthenopi', one of us might say, chiming a glass,
but the common measure of love is loss.
The cucumbers glistened in oil and thyme.

And here is the poet Alexander Hutchison reporting from the island of Rhodes on a picture of Greek women at outdoors work.

> In my hand this postcard of four women who cut and gather
> thin corn or dried grass stalks for plaiting. They work a line
> on a high headland with the sea behind them. One wears
> a short straw bonnet against the sun. Others have white
> headscarves wound round so little of their faces and none
> of the neck or throat shows. It's not enough to say that
> it must be hot work. They wear shirts, skirts, aprons
> and dresses of blue, grey, pink and white, with further
> binding to protect the skin at their forearms and wrists.
>
> It could be Rhodes; it might be Orkney, or fields above
> Cullen, after a dozen years of sudden climate change.
>
> They must pause and stretch, bind with some wisps
> and stoop again. Although they are posed and angled
> here a little, you can imagine it anytime, almost anywhere.
> It looks too hot for casual chat. A word or two perhaps
> on a longer easing stretch – anything else held
> back for whatever break they get and when.

This comes from Hutchison's 'Epistle from Pevkos', which combines prose and poetry, and was dedicated to the much loved Scottish poet Gael Turnbull, shortly after his death.

As John Ruskin and William Morris, those earnest nineteenth-century champions of useful work and opponents of useless toil, recognised, absorption in work is possible only if the work is fulfilling. This is what the poet Alexis Lykiard both acknowledges and celebrates in the following poem:

The Moment as Monument

An unremarkable middle-aged sculptress
(whose name I never meant to forget)
hews Paros marble. Dusty August air.

The years may have been lost now, yet
again I marvel at that statue's whiteness,
am witness to the strength of art that held her there

day after day, in a courtyard by the sea
struggling with stone and absolutely free.

And again on Rhodes, Lawrence Durrell (1912–90) watches a local fisherman who, like so many islanders, finds a way of living which combines work and sociability, the meagre returns of labour sweetened by the compensations of leisure.

Panagiotis of Lindos

Dark birds in nature redevise
Their linings every year: are not
The less like these weaving fishermen
Bent so exactly at their tattered seines
On a rotten wharf, their molten catch
Now sold and loaded: though they feather only
For fathoms of sea and the fishes within it,
Needles passing in a surf of lights.

Panagiotis has resigned it all
For an enamel can and olive shade:
His concern a tavern prospect,
Miles of sweet chestnut and borage.

This armament of wine he shares now
With the greatest philosopher, the least
Inventor, the meanest of doctrine of rest,
Mixing leisure and repose like wine and water,
Tutor and pupil in the crater.

His dark sleep is bruised by each
Sink of the sun below the castle
Where the Sporades have opened
Their spokes, and the whole Aegean
In brilliant soda turns the darkening bays.

Lindos, which straddles two bays, is one of three ancient cities on
Rhodes, the island where Durrell based himself for a while after the
end of the Second World War. From there he journeyed to other
islands in order to write his compendious account of Greek island
life. Hence the following, in which, again with a poet–novelist's
aborbed attentiveness, he watches

Dimitri of Carpathos

Four card-players: an ikon of the saint
On a pitted table among eight hands
That cough and spit or close like manacles
On fortunate court-cards or on the bottle
Which on the pitted paintwork stands.
Among them one whose soft transpontine nose
Fuller of dirty pores pricked on a chart
Has stood akimbo on the turning world,
From Cimbalu to Smyrna shaken hands,
Tasted the depths of every hidden sound:
In wine or poppy a drunkard with a drunkard's heart
Who never yet was known to pay his round.

Meanwhile below in harbour his rotten boat,
Bearded green from winter quarters, turns
Her scraggy throat to nudge the northern star,
And like a gypsy burns and burns; goes wild
Till something climbs the hill
And stands beside him at the tavern table
To pluck his drunken elbow like a child.
The toad, work, offering its arm.

In the following years, many foreigners, especially young ones from northern Europe and the United States, came to Greece in pursuit of the good life – which meant in practice cheap living, sun, sand, sea, sex, and an unwillingness to allow the political realities of the civil war and, later, the brutality, repression and bovine nastiness of colonels' junta, to cloud their vision of a hippie paradise. Not that all can stand accused of being blinded by the sun. And, anyway, Greece was, as it still is, beautiful, its climate greatly preferable to the rainy, cloud-filled skies of northern European countries, its inhabitants ostensibly courteous and open-hearted, though never, ever 'simple' (admittedly it takes time to crack open the clichés and discover the hidden darks, the wit and cunning of those who delight in adopting the expected pose); and for many years it was astonishingly cheap. The cheapness has gone, much else that brought the first backpackers remains, as they, some of them, remain, grown old in a way of life that had at first seemed a moment's choice but has now become their destiny. Something of this is evoked in Chris Hardy's 'I Work All Day'.

I Work All Day

I work all day
in this small bar
by the sea.

We start by sweeping
the floor and cleaning
the tables.

Then we serve breakfast,
carrying it across
from the kitchen.

The sun begins
to pour out heat
around midday.

We have to serve
soft drinks and juice
in the shade.

As the afternoon passes
we prepare so that when
the sun has fallen

down the insides of the sky
and approaches the mountain
we are ready for the people,

who sit silent when they watch
the horizon, and talk
when they watch each other.

Darkness appears
in the air like dye
in water.

Everyone is at the centre
of their own life,

a thing they cannot see

from the outside.
Even in the mirror
of a polished table

I do not see
my life, only a face
which seems to know

but will not tell
me what I am
or why.

Let's return to that bar
where the sun's evening light
burns on the mountain

that we will never visit.
We can take the children,
plan tomorrow

and the days after,
buy food on the way
and spend some time,

like emptying our pockets
for the waitress.
The money spent

does not come back
and our time like the sun's
liquid gold pours

into the cold tide
of the past that goes out
for ever.

ISLAND DEATH

Robert Frost has a gnomic two-liner called 'An Answer' that runs, 'But Islands of the Blessed, bless you, son,/I never came upon a blessed one.' If that is the answer, then what was the question? Presumably: Have you ever come across an earthly paradise, Mr Frost? Frost, his very name suggesting the imperishable substratum of cold that underlies all warmth, replies in the negative. The gentleman in the dustcoat waits as effectively behind a palm tree as beside a city piazza. This seems to be the meaning of 'The Isles of Greece' by Demetrios Capetanakis (1912–44).

> The sun is not in love with us,
> Nor the corrosive sea;
> Yet both will burn our dried-up flesh
> In deep intimacy.
>
> With stubborn tongues of briny death
> And heavy snakes of fire,
> Which writhe and hiss and crack the Greek
> Myth of the singing lyre.
>
> The dusty fig-tree cries for help,
> Two peasants kill one snake,
> While in our rocky heart the gods
> Of marble hush and break.
>
> After long ages all our love
> Became a barren fever,
> Which makes us glow in martyrdom
> More beautiful than ever.

Yet when the burning horses force
Apollo to dismount
And rest with us at least, he says
That beauty does not count.

In her Introduction to the slender collection of Capetanakis's poems, Edith Sitwell notes that in this, his last completed poem, Capetanakis 'tells us that all is vain – our love, and the life and death of the sun. Even our heroic suffering is in vain.' The year 1944 was an especially terrible time for Greece, but from the first there feels to have been a deep blackness in Greek consciousness. Certainly Odysseus's men discover that the island refuge of Circe harbours death. Their being turned into the swine is, at least in Christian mythography, taken to represent an image of death because it symbolises enslavement to sensual passion. Hence Eliot's line in 'Marina': 'those who sit in the stye of contentment, meaning/ Death'. There is, moreover, the actual death of their companion, Elpenor, who falls from the roof of Circe's dwelling, breaks his neck and is left unburied by the rest in their hurry to escape. He is the first shade Odysseus meets in the nether world; and he pleads for burial and for his oar to be planted over his grave. This is the *donnée* for a poem by the modern Greek poet, Takis Sinopoulos (1902–71), a mysteriously beautiful meditation on the continuity of Greece's past, legendary and historical, in its present.

Midday on the Island

Sea, stone, cypress,
the low shore devastated by salt and light,
rocks gnawed hollow by ravening wind and sun,
neither lift of water nor bird's wing,
only a thick, unwrinkled silence.

Then one of us, a young one at that, saw him.
Look, that must be him. We turned and
strange that we should know –
memories had dried like a stream in summer –
but yes, it was him, there, among the cypresses,
eye-pits empty,
gouging the sand with his blind finger-stubs.
Elpenor, I tried the name, *Elpenor,*
how did you get here, you were
dead when we left you, that iron stave
rammed through your side, blood
crusted on your lips as your heart stopped pumping.
We planted you at the sea's edge
to hear the wind and rough-tongued sea.
How come you're alive, how did you get here?

He didn't turn. I called again
scared, *Elpenor,*
don't you know my voice?
Is it you, old friend, did that rabbit's foot
save you after all to reach the boats?

Nothing. He never moved. Silence thickened.
Noon light drilled into earth, the sea, the rocks,
and Elpenor, hunched among dark cypresses,
dwindled and slowly thinned
into the wingless, echoless blue.

This translation is by the editor. It is a popular Greek belief that
ghosts walk at midday because the sun is then directly overhead so
that for this brief spell no shadow is cast by any person or thing.
Ghosts have no shadow.

In 1915 Rupert Brooke became a national hero in death. He was one of many British soldiers sent to fight in the ill-conceived attempt to wrest the Dardanelles from Turkish control, a misadventure that resulted in death or serious injury to thousands of Allied soldiers and sailors. Despite the assumption of most Australians, by no means all of these were Anzac troops, and despite an equally popular assumption in England, Brooke wasn't killed in battle. While on a troop-ship taking him through the Mediterranean he was bitten by a mosquito, septicaemia followed, and he was buried on the island of Skyros. Andrew Motion has a story of visiting the island as a very young man, and of seeing an army of ants march in orderly fashion out of Brooke's broken grave slab. The American poet, A. E. Stallings, who lives in Athens, also took the sea journey to Skyros, an event she records in her sonnet 'Visiting the Grave of Rupert Brooke':

> Rupert, this was where, I'm sure you knew,
> The sea nymph Thetis took Achilles to,
> And hid him, with his smooth cheek and gold curls,
> Amid the royal retinue of girls,
> As any mother might, to save her son,
> From war and death, by arrow or the gun.
> Odysseus, recruiting, in disguise,
> Set out for sale a range of merchandise,
> Stuffs no princess easily resists –
> Fine brocades, and bangles for the wrists,
> All manner of adornments, silver, gold,
> And set a blade among them, brazen, cold –
> A simple trap that might catch any boy.
> But only old men made it home from Troy.

> (from *Hapax*, 2006)

In Greece as elsewhere, islands are places of imprisonment. One island, in particular, Makronisos, became the prison home of thousands of Greeks who, having fought against the Nazis, found themselves after the war opposed to those who now assumed control of their nation. The great poet Yannis Ritsos (1909–90) was almost from the first in trouble with the authorities. In 1936, he had published *Epitaphios,* inspired by a photograph of a mother in Thessaloniki weeping over the body of her son, a striker from a tobacco factory, one of twelve who had been gunned down by police. The poem was publicly burnt by the Metaxas dictatorship and from then on until 1952, Nikos Stangos tells us, 'Ritsos was unable to publish freely, for political reasons.' At the time of the second civil war, Ritsos

> was sent for detention to Lemnos and then to the infamous 'Institute for National Re-education' on Makronisos, where the guards administered physical and psychological torture in an attempt to convert Communists into 'good Hellenes'. Finally, he was transferred to Agios Efstratios. Though released at last because of ill-health [he suffered from tuberculosis], he was picked up again in 1951 and detained for a further year . . . On Makronisos he placed his poems in a bottle which he buried in stony ground; on Agios Efstratios he was able to recite his works to fellow prisoners.

Among the poems that belong to this period is the famous 'Letter to Joliot-Curie' and many short lyrics, in one of which he says, 'No one will silence our song. We sing on.' Hence,

Unexpropriated

They came. They were looking at the ruins, the
                                    surrounding plots of land,
they seemed to measure something with their eyes, they tasted

the air and the light on their tongues. They liked it.
Surely they wanted to take something away from us. We
buttoned up our shirts, although it was hot,
and looked at our shoes. Then one of us
pointed with his finger to something in the distance. The
                                                                others turned.

As they were turned, he bent discreetly,
took a handful of soil, hid it in his pocket
and moved away indifferently. When the strangers turned about
they saw a deep hole before their feet,
they moved, they looked at their watches and they left.
In the pit: a sword, a vase, a white bone.

(translated by Nikos Stangos)

Who are 'They'? Outsiders, certainly, people who want to take 'something away from us', whether that be freedom, land, identity, history, whatever of Greece they can appropriate. Ritsos's refusal to be specific is essential to the poem's meaning. Modern Greek history is a tragic catalogue of violent oppression from enemies outside or within. But always there is, too, a refusal to submit, despite the appearance of doing so – 'We buttoned up our shirts', which also hints at concealment as well as a deep sense of Greece as a nation whose spirit of resistance is undefeatable. When the strangers see what is in the pit, 'A sword, a vase, a white bone', they leave. History may reduce to a few objects discoverable by archaeologists, but here such objects symbolise or at least hint at what will meet all attempted acts of appropriation: resistence and death.

Perhaps the greatest of all modern Greek poets, George Seferis (1900–71), though politically apart from Ritsos, shared his sense of a 'Greekness', ironically enough called 'Romiosini', which is inextricable from the nation's language, the land, the sea, the islands, the history of Greece. The goons and thugs of the 1967–74 Junta hoped that Seferis, who in 1963 had been awarded the Nobel Prize for Literature, would confer some legitimacy on them, but no such luck. He refused to publish any poems while they were in power. At the very end of his life he did, though, write a poem 'On Aspalathoi', which though its setting is the bay of Sounion rather than an island, merits inclusion here:

Sounion was lovely that spring day –
the feast of the Annunciation.
Sparse green leaves around rust-coloured stone,
red earth, and aspalathoi
with their huge thorns and their yellow flowers
already out.
In the distance the ancient columns, strings of a harp
                                                still vibrating . . .

Peace.
– What would have made me think of Ardiaios?
Possibly a word in Plato, buried in the mind's furrows:
the name of the yellow bush
hasn't changed since his time.
That evening I found the passage:
'They bound him hand and foot,' it says,
'they flung him down and flayed him,
they dragged him along
gashing his flesh on thorny aspalathoi,
and they went and threw him into Tartarus, torn to shreds.'

In this way Ardiaios, the terrible Pamphylian tyrant,
paid for his crimes in the nether world.

31 March 1971

(translated by Edmund Keeley and Philip Sherrard)

Seferis gives the date of the poem because it is part of its meaning. Springtime is the time of rebirth. Tyrants, whether ancient or modern, will be overthrown and Greece will yet again renew itself. The temple to Poseidon at Sounion was still unfinished when the Persians destroyed it in 480 BC, but later in that very year the might of the Persian navy was crushed at the sea battle of Salamis. And there is a further possible frisson in that Pamphylia was an ancient Greek colony in Asia Minor; it may be that Seferis intends a glance at the disaster of the 1922–3 campaign and future restitution. Whether that will ever be achieved seems increasingly unlikely. For the foreseeable future, at all events, Istanbul will continue to exist under the Turkish flag. But three years after Seferis's death, the modern versions of Ardiaios were overthrown and democracy was restored to Greece.

In most island cemeteries, upholders and opponents of centuries of tyranny lie side by side. The necropolis, customarily set some way outside the town, will be surrounded by whitewashed walls; as often as not a cypress at each corner smokes up into the blue Aegean sky, and the marble tombs, crammed up against each other, usually feature oil lamps whose glimmering, shimmering flames seem at night as though a field of stars has fallen to earth and finds itself at ease in its new surroundings. Something of this is caught in Matt Simpson's poem, 'Moonlight on Aegina'.

> My mind keeps doubling back
> to that snug back-lane necropolis,
> with its firefly night-lights
> quivering on marble tombs
> set out like tables at a wedding,
> whose last guests left an hour ago.
>
> The Greeks don't see their dead
> as really dead. And who can blame them?

forfeiting all that passionate light,
purples, cobalts, sapphire skies,
jasper, turquoise seas. So how
could they ever be happy in
a nothing-doing blind eternity?

Persephone and Dis go hotly at it
down below. And doesn't she
come flouncing back for half a year?
Bones are buried treasure. They defy
something that always wants to be denied.

And there's always the moon
to put an unresenting face on things.

I keep homing in on that cemetery
as a place not to be afraid in, a place
of love still, asking you to imagine
that death is not an end but a continuing,
not just of atoms that disperse
and randomly regroup, but of obstinate
redounding memory

perhaps of strolling back, tipsy with talk
from a lingered-in taverna, and walking
among these graves with the sea –
thalassa! thalassa! – two hundred yards away
down a wine-dark jasmine-scented lane.

But Greek islands also house the war dead, and the island of
Leros, as mentioned, has cemeteries for those soldiers of different
nationalities – British, German, Italian – who fought and died there
during the Second World War. The Battle of Leros and its dead are
commemorated in the following poem by Dimitris Tsaloumas:

Anniversary

Battle of Leros – November 1943

We both laughed that time
when I stepped off the back gate
above the stony ditch into the dark
and the dead soldier's gut,
who lay ripening like a fig
in the off-season heat of those
late autumn days.

That was fifty-four years ago,
too long a time you might say
for any stench to endure. Yet though
I've discarded my boots since
and washed by feet clean,
it has established itself in cavities
within the porous soul –
a standard, so to speak, by which
all smell and flavour's judged,
degree of pungency and smoothness
of sauce and condiment
or fragrance of woman's flesh.

A conquest surely, though that night
we laughed the way youth does
at things beyond its speech,
and maybe this boast can now be made
because words age tough, their touch
too coarse for the silk thread
into the maze back.

Yet as I write
a rose, brother, a big red rose

burns on his livid cheek
and I think of you in its glow
and hear sweet voices singing
that could be angels in the trees.
For nothing stirs abroad
on this bleak night but leaves,
and the ditch is full of rain.

And in a poem from his 1972 collection, ominously entitled
Muffled, Yannis Ritsos provides stark evidence of the horror of
violence on the prison island of Makronisos during the period of the
Junta, when he himself was immured there.

Concentration Camp

The whistle, the cry, the swishing, the thud;
the reversed water, the smoke, the stone, the saw;
a fallen tree among the killed men; –
when the guards undressed them, you could hear falling
one by one from their pockets the telephone tokens,
the small pair of scissors, the nail-clipper, the little mirror
and the long, hollow wig of the bald hero
strewn with straw, broken glass and thorns
and a cigarette-butt hidden behind the ear.

Naxos was one of the first islands to work in marble. It supplied
the lions for Delos and also went in for sculpting larger-than-lifesize
nude youths. Two of these, being flawed, were left in the quarries
where they were made, and one is the subject of Chris Hardy's
poem 'Definitely Human', which depicts a kouros (naked youth) I
myself have seen and marvelled at: the compelling image of death-
in-life or is it life-in-death?

Definitely Human

Kouros, Flerio, Naxos

I expected him to be
pushed aside beneath a wall
out of the farmer's way
but he was abandoned
head down on a slope
half over on his side
looking stunned
not my fault
I only had the one,
definitely human.

Before he was complete
he left home
on the mountain, ruled
by eagles and the wind,
to cross the ocean
and reach the city,
where he would be
adored, caressed,
become a man
full grown, definitely human.

But he slipped
out of line
and cracked.
I can't explain
how I arrived here
from where I began
any more than he can.

Imperfect, broken,
young, definitely human.

No one could
heal his face
frozen in a blind
stone sleep.
Slumped, feet up
for the millennia to come,
thoughtless as a rock,
warm to touch in the sun,
definitely human.

I haven't seen the Samian Kouros that forms the subject of Nadine Brummer's compelling poem, but the speculative, considered weight she brings to her meditation evokes much of the Greek sense of the paradox of living stone, of the human hacked from inert matter.

The Samian Kouros

Can't read his lips
Level with his hips
I see scrotum and fingertips

which larger than lifesize
clench by his thighs
and resemble mine

in that posture
of wanting to touch ... there
and there .... I stare

at the youth's behind –
two concentric lines
select buttocks most finely.

They could be natural mounds
not marble, veined
and cut. Underground

more bodies may lie
ready to be picked up like
this five-metres-high

kouros. Only imagine
the proclivities of stone
to shape into someone

if given time. I've read
that molluscs on the sea-bed
needed millenia to build

first, their own defences
then, from their ruined shells,
white cliffs.

And him? Read his eyes –
their wide, blind gaze
outsees our horizons.

He stands as if
he knows the stuff
he's made from, his tough

chemistry. Feel flesh,
think how it's stressed
in reproduction, of our duresse

in being real.
Now consider the ordeal
by fire that marble,

or rather, limestone
went through to become
granular, crystalline,

before compacted
into blocks, hacked
from a quarry and worked

into the serious weight
of genitalia and gait
of hero. He is right

to smile slightly for when,
or if he is wholly broken,
his dust will be stone again.

This beautiful, teasing meditation on metamorphosis acknowledges, as how could it not, death as part of temporality. Even those who embark for Cythera must discover that death awaits them. *Et in Arcadia ego.*

TRAVELLING ON

However far an island may seem from the cares of temporal existence, however far from the aches of mortality, however temptingly it signals a release from censorious dailiness, once it has been discovered and grown familiar, the allure of the refuge where Calypso awaits can pall. Better then to keep journeying. This is what C. P. Cavafy recommends in one of the greatest of modern Greek poems.

Ithaka

As you set out for Ithaka
hope your road is a long one,
full of adventure, full of discovery.
Laistrygonians, Cyclops,
angry Poseidon – don't be afraid of them:
you'll never find things like that on your way
as long as you keep your thoughts raised high,
as long as a rare sensation
touches your spirit and your body.
Laistrygonians, Cyclops,
wild Poseidon – you won't encounter them
unless you bring them along inside your soul,
unless your soul sets them up in front of you.

Hope your road is a long one.
May there be many summer mornings when,
with what pleasure, what joy,
you enter harbours you're seeing for the first time;
may you stop at Phoenician trading stations

to buy fine things,
mother-of -pearl and coral, amber and ebony,
sensual perfume of every kind –
as many sensual perfumes as you can;
and may you visit many Egyptian cities
to learn and go on learning from those who know.

Keep Ithaka always in your mind.
Arriving there is what you're destined for.
But don't hurry the journey at all.
Better the journey if it lasts for years,
so you're old by the time you reach the island,
wealthy with all you've gained on the way,
not expecting Ithaka to make you rich.

Ithaka gave you the marvellous journey.
Without her you wouldn't have set out.
She has nothing left to give you now.

(C. P. Cavafy, *Collected Poems,* 1984
translated by Edmund Keeley & Philip Sherrard
edited by George Savidis)

Reasons for delay, motives for deferral. But other promptings urge travellers to their destination, the joy proposed. Once arrived, though, time will not relent. Seven days may soon pass but seven years can drag. Was Odysseus really compelled to renew his wanderings or was that a story he made up to excuse his desire to be gone? Although there is no hard evidence to support my hunch, I have always thought that the setting of Robert Browning's two lyrics 'Meeting at Night' and 'Parting at Morning' is an island. There is the eroticism of the secretive meeting, of 'two hearts beating each to each!' after the man's impetuous night-time arrival by boat. 'I gain the cove with pushing prow,/And quench its speed i' the slushy sand.' But come morning,

> Round the cape of a sudden came the sea,
> And the sun looked over the mountain's rim:
> And straight was a path of gold for him,
> And the need of a world of men for me.

Phoebus Apollo's peremptory lighting of a straight path acts as a call to action. 'The need of a world of men for me.' The pacey anapaests are followed by the grandly affirmative stresses on 'men' and 'me'. This the world my daylight self needs and must have. It could be Odysseus speaking.

'*Don't leave. Stay,*' whisper the islands in David Mason's poem 'In Transit', but the whisperings cannot still 'the turmoil of desire'.

> The urge to settle never stays for long,
> nor does desire to move like a windblown seed
> when days have no more purpose than a song
> at midnight, drifting from the olive trees,
> or books you packed but cannot seem to read.
> The passing stranger is well known in Greece.
>
> Once in Athens you rode the crowded bus,
> watching the dull eyes of those who aimed for work
> through gritty streets, the traffic's heave and thrust.
> Elsewhere the perfect sculpture of the light
> reminded you what leaves us in the dark.
> No Baedeker explained your jaded sight.
>
> Islands, more islands than you could name,
> lay like lovers at morning. *Don't leave. Stay.*
> But the only Eden that could ever claim
> you wholly disappeared beneath the waves.
> Revise, tomorrow, what you write today,
> as tides reform in mouths of the sea caves.

A fisherman's fantasy, after all –
sun-dazed, wine-dazed – with a flick of her fins
dives out of sight, ignoring his fervent call
while his boat nods *yes* on the dancing sea.
Here all the turmoil of desire begins.
You are as happy as you'll ever be.

Of course the traveller may have regrets. Staying cloys the
appetite with what is fed on; leaving sharpens the feeling of loss.
This is the mixed burden of the Australian poet Jan Owen's 'Salt', a
poem describing the view of Poros town as the ferry she is on curves
away from the island on the return journey of the Saronic run that
will take in stops at Methana, an isthmus of the mainland, then the
island of Aegina, before it reaches its final destination, Piraeus.

> The sea is sibilant as Greek,
> the wind draws tears.
> Happiness, that side effect,
> is steaming away
> with the banked-up foam
> from the stern of the ferry,
> turbulent hydra spume.
> Twenty or thirty gulls litter the wake of air,
> shrieking you back like harpies
> to their gold-white clawhold in time,
> an island's farewell pose.
> The gap-toothed men untangling nets
> on their thrifty beach are sliding away,
> the cats that shadow milky walls
> and chimney pots,
> Toula fierce with a broom,
> smiling Christos stacking pita,
> the children selling bait on the steps,

are gone with their pell-mell lanes.
The windows round the waterfront
make an amphitheatre of eyes
fixed on your vanishing point
in a sea grown huge as longing.
Like an easy birth into a dream
Poros is rounding over the rim.
Formal and far away –
a small iced cake on a bright blue cloth.
Dipping below the shoreline last
Is the centred clock-tower spire
a candle for the one you were.

Regret also tinges 'Trizonia', a wittily observant poem by the English poet Angela Kirby. Its one long sentence unspools over twenty-six lines as memories run higgledy-piggledy into rhythm's mesh.

Trizonia

O most excellent donkey who,
not having heard of the sleep button,
woke me three times this morning
with your ancient and execrable lament,
do you bemoan the start
of your overburdened day
and the end of your brief night's rest
in this unpromising patch of scrub
or do you, perhaps, grieve for me
who must today leave this incomparable islet
where there are neither cars
nor motorcycles, where nothing
very much happens, apart
from the occasional birth or marriage

and the rather more frequent deaths,
where there is little to see, just Iannis
repainting the peeling mermaid
on his taverna, and his grandmother
taking a broom to the six hollow-ribbed cats
who have stolen yet another chicken-leg,
and the three old men who,
having finished their backgammon
and the last of the ouzo, now take
the sun's path home across the harbour
in a boat as blue as that clump of scabious
you are considering?

For the poet Philip Gardner, leaving Cyprus, where he had served
much of his national service, was far less of a wrench, though not to
be managed without a sense of loss. The following lines come from
the end of his long poem 'Leaving the Island', written at the end of
the 1950s.

Must what is life become mere history?
This island, that has contained me for a year
Like an adopted village, where the names
Are learnt, then fall from the tongue without a prompt,
– Will leaving turn it to another date
Contained within the mind – shrunk to a speck
In seas of time stretching on either hand,
Small as the islands glimpsed from aeroplanes?
Will memory keep it warm as in a thermos,
Or will it rust, a branch-line of the mind,
Choked with the weeds and nettles of neglect?

The light's last sparks glint in the old cathedral's
Celluloid windows; dusk fills the huge moat
Clogged with trees like mushrooms; shadows hide

The empty spaces of grass, the ruined churches.
A yellow beacon on the harbour wall
Shines palely on the bay: the fishing-boats
Drawn up in tranquil lines on the glass calm,
The dockside clean, warehouses swept and empty
(My peaceful heart, eased of its weight of words);
And ships, with other ports upon their bows,
Waiting the morning and the casting-off.

Kirby's is unashamedly the viewpoint of the casual visitor, Gardner has more invested, though his Englishness is not to be doubted. 'Dusk brims the shadows', Larkin had written in 'At Grass'. 'Dusk fills the huge moat', Gardner notes, although I doubt that any Greek would characterise the sudden sweeping in of Mediterranean dark as 'dusk', that 'darker stage of twilight' according to the Oxford English Dictionary.

Still, night-time leavings have their appeal, as the English poet Chris Hardy testifies in his poem about the urge to travel on.

Somewhere to Go

All harbours are beautiful
full of iron and space

their own horizon
and a dome of light.

At Mandraki beneath the windmills
we sat above the oily blue

with the slight fine air
of salted sewage

looking at the great walls
before the city

the liners and tankers
yachts from Hamilton

gin palaces from Ostia
fishing boats poking about

for a place
the arriving, leaving

and waiting.
Then, walking up the lane

behind the kiosks and go-downs
we found a shop just shutting

and bought green olives
a lump of bread and some apricots.

Back on deck waiting
you were tired and bored

*is this what you've been
going on about?*

But the sea is calm
around our white bow

the luggage stacked
our captain idles.

Beyond the point
the north wind

which blows all summer
is making the hydrofoils

bellyflop and crawl
this is the best place to be

always, bags packed and
somewhere to go.

HOMEWARD BOUND

As he prepares to leave his island, Prospero promises his brother they will have 'calm seas, auspicious gales' and expeditious sail. But Prospero is of course eager to be gone. Few travellers leave a Greek island without regret, though this can be, often is, blended with other emotions. For Iain Crichton Smith, the story of Odysseus' journey home becomes a metaphor for open-ended submission to the chances life brings.

Next Time

Listen, when you come home
to see your wife again
where the tapestry stands unfinished
across the green brine,
sit among the stones
and consider how it was
in the old days
before you became a king
and walked hunchbacked
with decisions on your shoulders.

Sit among the rocks
hearing the sound of the sea
eternally unchanging
and watch the buttercups
so luminously pale.

The cries of the dead
haunt the gaunt headland

and the shields clash
in that astonishing blue.

Simply enter the boat
and leave the island
for there is no return,
boy, forerunnner of kings.

Next time, do this,
salt-bronzed veteran,
let the tapestry be unfinished
as truthful fiction is.

David Mason also intuits during his sea journey at Easter back to
Piraeus from the island of Kos – a journey that takes you past the
island of Patmos – the possibility of mystery, of the ineffable.

Gulls in the Wake

Late in our journey from the pier at Kos
I had come up for air. Most passengers
had found their bunks or drunk themselves asleep
in the comfy bar. Adrift and floodlit,

I let suspended time wash over me,
its kitchen smells, salt wind and plodding engines,
as two guys swinging beer cans walked the deck,
singing the liturgy. *Christ is risen!*

Drunken, genuinely happy, they waved
across cool space at constellated lights
of villages, and greeted me, a stranger.
I answered, *Truly, He is risen,* though

I don't believe it. Not risen for this world.
Not here. Not now.
Then I heard cadences
of priestly chanting from an Athens church
broadcast to any pilgrim still awake.

Who could explain an unbeliever's joy
as rockets flared from the coast near Sounion
and music ferried death to life out there,
untethered in the dark?

And that was when I saw them – ghostly, winged,
doggedly following outside our light,
hopeful without a thought of hope, feeding
and diving to feed in waves I could not see.

'Christ is risen,' Greek people say to one another on Easter
Sunday; and they answer one another, 'Truly, He is risen.'

But the most beautiful of these poems about the homeward
journey, and a suitable poem with which to bring this anthology to
its close, is David Constantine's 'Watching for Dolphins', which
ends with travellers ready to rejoin the many-peopled life of the
modern city, the allure of the Aegean and its islands now left
behind and with it the ancientness of 'cymbal, gong and drum',
Constantine's measured take on Yeats's more strident account of
'that dolphin-torn, that gong-tormented sea'. And though the
island from which Constantine sails is almost certainly Aegina, the
nearest to Piraeus of the Saronic islands, knowing this is in no way
essential to an appreciation of his poem.

Watching for Dolphins

In the summer months on every crossing to Piraeus
One noticed that certain passengers soon rose
From seats in the packed saloon and with serious
Looks and no acknowledgement of a common purpose
Passed forward through the small door into the bows
To watch for dolphins. One saw them lose

Every other wish. Even the lovers
Turned their desires on the sea, and a fat man
Hung with equipment to photograph the occasion
Stared like a saint, through sad bi-focals; others,
Hopeless themselves, looked to the children for they
Would see dolphins if anyone would. Day after day

Or on their last opportunity all gazed
Undecided whether a flat calm were favourable
Or a sea the sun and the wind between them raised
To a likeness of dolphins. Were gulls a sign, that fell
Screeching from the sky or over an unremarkable place
Sat in a silent school? Every face

After its character implored the sea.
All, unaccustomed, wanted epiphany,
Praying the sky would clang and the abused Aegean
Reverberate with cymbal, gong and drum.
We could not imagine more prayer, and had they then
On the waves, on the climax of our longing come

Smiling, snub-nosed, domed like satyrs, oh
We should have laughed and lifted children up
Stranger to stranger, pointing how with a leap

They left their element, three or four times, centred
On grace, and heavily and warm re-entered,
Looping the keel. We should have felt them go

Further and further into the deep parts. But soon
We were among the great tankers, under their chains
In black water. We had not seen the dolphins
But woke, blinking. Eyes cast down
With no admission of disappointment the company
Dispersed and prepared to land in the city.

I can't, however, let the matter quite rest here. 'Watching for
Dolphins' is the title poem of a collection published in 1983. Some
fifteen years later, the poet Matt Simpson was staying with me in
the small flat on Aegina my wife and I have on a long-term rent. The
flat is in the village of Faros, some fifteen minutes walk along the
shore road from Aegina's port town and capital. ('Faros' means
'lighthouse' but, this being Greece, there is naturally no lighthouse
at Faros.) One afternoon, Matt and I were sitting on a low sea-wall
just outside the town, gazing across the water to the small island of
Angistri. 'Do you ever see dolphins here?' Matt asked. 'No,' I told
him, which was the truth. Farther down the Saronic run, yes. I'd
seen them following in the wake of a boat that some years earlier
had taken us to the island of Spetses. Here, though, they had
vanished. At all events I'd not seen one in years of looking. But as I
spoke five dolphins suddenly rose out of the sea, dived, rose again,
and so continued until they disappeared round the headland to our
left. Hence, the following poem of Matt's:

The Day We Saw Dolphins

The day we saw dolphins
persuaded me some god
should be acknowledged.

How else explain
the synchronicity

of giving each other
the same gift? Hadn't you said

how rarely dolphins swam
around the island now,

regretting what I'd miss,
might never share? Then

suddenly Look! I yelled,

out in the shimmering bay,
five, yes, five broad backs

sewing the turquoise sea
to a dusky purple sky.

How else describe the joy I felt,
the joy I saw in you,

your wished-for possibility,
my discovering it?

And with this poem and the following wish, we can bring the
anthology to its close. May you see dolphins!

Acknowledgements

We would like to thank all of the authors for making this collection possible by allowing us to use their material, and gratefully acknowledge permission to reprint copyright material as follows:

Glyn Hughes for permission to use an extract from 'Life Class'; Iakovos Kampanelis for permission to use 'Naxos'; Philip Ramp for permission to use 'On the *Flying Dolphin* to Aegina: An Elegy'; Nadine Brummer for permission to use 'End of Holiday (Ikaria, 2002)', 'Olive Trees' and 'The Samian Kouros'; Richard Berengarten for use of part of 'Holding the Sea' and for 'for Anastassis Vistonitis'; George Gomori for use of 'Island in the Mediterranean', and Clive Wilmer for his translation of it; Anita Sullivan for permission to use 'On Ikaria' and 'Paradise' and some extracts from *Ikaria: A Love Odyssey on a Greek Island*, published by Burning Daylight in 2008; Shoestring Press for permission to use 'Olives', 'Cicadas', 'Scottish Waiter Bringing Squid', 'Moonlight on Aegina' and 'The Day We Saw Dolphins' by Matt Simpson; Dimitris Tsaloumas for permission to use 'Aubade for the Lady of Ships', 'The Threshing-Floor' and 'Anniversary'; Chris Hardy for permission to use 'Just in Case', 'I Work All Day', 'Definitely Human' and 'Somewhere to Go'; Alan Dixon for permission to use 'At the Poseidon'; Deryn Rees-Jones for permission to use 'Morning Song' by Michael Murphy; Stratis Paschalis for permission to use 'The Farmhouse' in a translation by John Lucas from *One for the Piano*; Alexis Lykiard for permission to use 'The Moment as Monument'; Redbeck Press for permission to use 'Midday on the Island' by Takis Sinopoulos in a translation by John Lucas; Angela Kirby for use of 'Trizonia'; Philip Gardner for lines from his long poem 'Leaving the Island'; Rachel Hadas for permission to use 'Samian Morning, 1971'; Charles Fishman for permission to use 'Andros Night'; David Mason for permission to use 'Acrostic from Aegina', 'In Transit' and 'Gulls in the Wake'; A. E. Stallings for permission to use 'The Wife of the Man of Many Wiles' (from *Archaic Smile*, University of Evansville Press, 1999) and 'Visiting the Grave of Rupert Brooke' (from *Hapax*, Northwestern University Press, 2006); Jan Owen for permission to use 'Salt'; Michael Waters for permission to use 'Parthenopi'; Sandy Hutchison for permission to use extracts from 'Epistle from Pevkos'; the Estate of Michael Ayrton for permission to reproduce lines from *Testament of Daedalus*; Katerina Anghelaki-Rooke for permission to use 'The Other Penelope' and 'Heat', and Jackie Willcox for permission to use her translation of 'Heat'; Bloodaxe for permission to use 'Odysseus and the Sou'wester' from Jen Hadfield's collection *Nigh-No-Place*; HarperCollins Australia for permission to use an extract from *The Sponge Divers* by Charmian Clift and George Johnston; Princeton University Press for permission to use 'In the Manner of G.S.' and 'On Aspalathoi' by George Seferis, both translated by Edmund Keeley and Philip Sherrard from his *Collected Poems*; Enitharmon Press for permission to use 'A Further Frontier' by David Gascoyne from his *Selected Poems*; Faber & Faber for permission to use lines from 'Tithonus' by Paul Muldoon from *Horse Latitudes*; Faber & Faber for permission to use 'Delos (Temple of Isis)' by Constantine Trypanis from his collection *Pompeian Dog*; Bloodaxe for permission to use 'Honey from Palaiochora' and 'Watching for Dolphins' from *Collected Poems* by David Constantine; Bloodaxe for permission to use Josephine Balmer's translations from *Sappho: Poems & Fragments* and *Classical Women Poets*; Faber & Faber for permission to use 'Panagiotis of Lindos' and 'Dimitri of Carpathos' by Lawrence Durrell; Princeton University Press for permission to use 'Ithaka' by Constantine Cavafy, translated by Edmund Keeley and Philip Sherrard, from his *Collected Poems*; Carcanet for permission to publish 'Next Time' by Iain Crichton Smith.

Index of First Lines

Index of Poem Titles

Index of Poets